SEMIOTEXT(E) ACTIVE AGENTS SERIES

© 2021 Dodie Bellamy

All rights reserved. No part of this book may be reproduced, stored in a retrieval system, or transmitted by any means, electronic, mechanical, photocopying, recording, or otherwise, without prior permission of the publisher.

Published by Semiotext(e)
PO BOX 629, South Pasadena, CA 91031
www.semiotexte.com

Special thanks to Bradford Nordeen, Ella Blanchon, Paul Monroe and Lia Gangitano.

Cover: Greer Lankton, *Aunt Ruth*, 1980–83. © The Estate of Greer Lankton.
Design: Hedi El Kholti

ISBN: 978-1-63590-157-3
Distributed by The MIT Press, Cambridge, Mass. and London, England
Printed in the United States of America

BEE REAVED

Dodie Bellamy

semiotext(e)

"We are here and you are where you are."
— Nick Cave

Contents

HERE

Hoarding as *Écriture*	11
Leaky Boundaries	24
The Violence of the Image	30
The Pink Place	49
The Endangered Unruly	52
Laugh and Cry: On Ugo Rondinone's Clowns (with Kevin Killian)	63
Cinderella Syndrome	69
Unbearable Intimacies	80
Pushing and Pulling, Pulling and Pushing (with Kevin Killian)	86
The Kingdom of Isolation	91
The Ghosts We Live With	103

WHERE

On Becoming Undone	109
Photo Op	113
Kevin and Dodie (with Kevin Killian)	117
Anniversary	153
Jeffree	157
Bee Reaved	162
Plague Widow	172
Chase Scene	187
Acknowledgments	251

HERE

1

Hoarding as *Écriture*

"[O]ne does fill some with all one takes in, and I've taken in, I dare say, more than I've natural room for."
— Henry James, *The Ambassadors*

In August, 2015, Kevin Killian and I turned over fifty-five file boxes of ephemera to the Beinecke Rare Book & Manuscript Library at Yale. Negotiations for the transfer, like those in a hostage situation, were long and drawn out, and we didn't know until a month before it happened if the deal was going to go through. So for two years Kevin and I had this big secret we dared only to whisper to a couple of our closest friends—and we still have a big secret because telling anybody how much money we received is considered beyond vulgar. This is painful for both of us. Though we spent thirty years of our literary life hoarding its dejecta, our writing has been committed to spewing all sorts of shit few would dare reveal. Hoarders of information we have never been.

Kevin and I don't have a lot of space. We live in a one bedroom apartment, with a small back porch we use for an office. We used to keep dozens of boxes of whatever in the basement, but one day our landlord made everybody clean out all their stuff, and it's sort of ruined our lives. Even with a storage unit three blocks away, boxes are stacked everywhere. The storage unit was so full that in order to organize our archives, we rented a second unit for a year. The artist Kota Ezawa also lent us his studio when he was on an extended out-of-town gig. I feel abject and scattered when I take in the disorganized chaos that surrounds me. Books have overflown their shelves and are stacked in irregular, toppling piles on every available surface. We're getting rid of half these books, we declare. The last time we did a book sweep we made $500, but the will to do another sweep never seems to arise. It's both more and less than laziness; its the sheer intensity of decision-making that stops us. That book on Surrealism I've had since high school—to remove it would be like tossing away a part of my DNA. Same with my two copies of Julia Kristeva's *Powers of Horror*—even though the parts that matter most to me have long been scanned and stored in the PDF folder on my hard drive, which is backed up both locally and online. As long as there's an internet and I have money to pay for it, *Powers of Horror* will never leave me. But when I touch the books, I'm flooded with memories of discovering the lack around which all my writing would henceforth revolve, my brain sparking, my hand scribbling in the margins, purple, red, black. If I got rid of my two copies of *Powers of Horrors*—even though I know I'll never read either again—it would be as if I were rejecting my younger self, saying to my younger self *I never really valued you.*

Way back in the '70s my younger self read an interview with the novelist Jayne Anne Phillips—this was before Phillips started publishing with mainstream presses—and I remember her talking about the junk piled around the houses of poor people in the South, how by surrounding themselves with all this broken-down stuff, people who had nothing could feel the comfort of surplus. She somehow connected the lushness of Southern writing to those junkyard houses. I think of the stylistic opulence of my first novel, *The Letters of Mina Harker*, all the sex, cultural references, quotes, puns, poetry, parody I crammed on top of one another—each convoluted sentence screams THESE WORDS MATTER DODIE MATTERS. If only I'd kept my copy of Jayne Anne Phillips' first chapbook of stories, *Sweethearts*, printed in 1976 in an edition of 400. I bet it would be worth something now. That's the problem with choosing—it cannot be trusted. Invariably, non-hoarding lets you down.

Archivists wine and dine and flatter you until they break through your defenses. It's like the archivists are Mommy and you're sitting on the toilet taking your first poo. They say, "Good Dodie!" and you give them whatever they want, even tender bits you know are better kept hidden. What archivists want are singular unique objects, the irreplaceable. All these letters, photos, contracts, yellowed news clippings, flyers, manuscripts—moving my hands across their object auras, the sadness of materiality strikes me, the inevitability of loss. I think of old people getting ready to die and giving away their stuff. I think of schizophrenics who get rid of everything they own, all their money, and set off. I unearth the first two pages of a letter so intense it verges on love letter, but the final page is missing and I can't figure out who it possibly could have been from. Dismay hits me, this sense of a vast past that has vaporized—all that love and anger and realization. My past. The more the papers are organized, I start to think of them as an exoskeleton protecting me from annihilation. The sense of exposure is unbearable. I feel like I'm attending my own wake; I feel like I'm being embalmed. But I bear it because I want the money, want to be remembered—even though the future the archives promise feels impossible. Impossible in that I won't be here any longer, impossible in that anybody would be interested in my life/stuff. And then there's my apocalyptic pessimism—it's hard to believe that human life won't soon be extinct. Posterity, despite the Beinecke's climate-controlled storage facilities, may end up being puny. I gave the archivists everything. Everything except my journals and wedding photos and anything to do with my deceased parents. I kept these tokens out of love and a conviction that I'm not finished yet.

Sometimes I run into someone I know I don't get along with, but I can't remember why. An impression too vague to base behavior or attitude on, yet there it is between us, foggy as scratched Plexiglas. A woman I haven't seen for a decade sticks her face in mine and gives a fulsome apology for some previous bad behavior, and in a fit of claustrophobic panic I find myself saying *don't worry about it, everything's fine, it was a long time ago, I'm as much to blame as you*—even though I have no idea what she's talking about. Friends who teach complain that these *young people* have no sense of history, but I worry that no one can escape our ahistorical zeitgeist, that all of us are tunneling towards a totalizing NOW. I imagine existence as a boundless expanse of dirt and I'm a worm burrowing through it, gorging on it on one end, shitting it out on the other. I read online that the donut shape is the basic organizing structure of multi-celled creatures, that the human body is an elongated donut, our digestive tube from mouth to anus, the donut's hole. Our deepest interiority is a slick pink hole. Whatever I haven't written down slips away. My journals prove that I have existed, that I'm a continuation of *something*. Dozens of volumes of fleeting thoughts and emotions—much of it embarrassing and not nearly enough description—waiting for a crack of light, waiting to be shaped, loved.

I worry about my mother's photos—hundreds of them that after eight years are still too poignant for me to sort through—maybe

I should have given them to the archive. What if my cultural capital plummets and nobody wants a second batch of my residue. I imagine myself dying alone in a hovel, undetected until neighbors complain about the smell and my starving cats have eaten away my face. My disgruntled landlord, to whom I owe back rent, tosses my belongings into a dumpster, and my mother's snapshots grow soggy—all her smiling relatives and friends—even I don't know who many of them are—their meaning, their index disintegrating. In the archive they'd rest in boxes of acid-free files, waiting for a curious grad student to unearth them, to plunge their obscurities. Writing students have told me that in other classes they've been admonished not to describe photographs because that's boring—but I never tire of writing about them, of staring and staring until I feel like I'm passing through the emulsion and holding a beating heart. Kevin gave all his prints— thirty years' worth of portraits of literary types—to the Beinecke. He scanned them beforehand, so he figured he wasn't really losing anything. But I mourn the loss of analogue photo processes. In order to peer *into* digital images, I envision them pixelated behind a shadow emulsion. This imagined emulsion links the iPhone-clicking Dodie to the darkroom-in-her-closet Dodie of my twenties, to the work-study job I had at Indiana University's photo lab, hand-printing group photos from events held on campus. In a darkened room white paper is inseminated with light then sloshed in a bath of toxic chemicals, its image slowly materializing. Since an image appeared so long after its capture, it always surprised. The film *Blow-Up* is a tribute to the mystery of the image, its power to hold secrets. Only through hyperfocused surrender can one unveil its prize.

In college I was taught that emulsion was comprised of silver halide crystals dispersed in gelatin rendered from cows fed mustard, which resonated with the Knox gelatin that ladies of my childhood dissolved in hot water and chugged to make their nails grow strong. It was Rose Knox who marketed gelatin to women. After her husband died in 1908, friends urged her to sell the business, but Mrs. Knox cared too deeply about women and gelatin and her workers to do that. When she took over as CEO, she instituted a five-day work week, two weeks of paid vacation, and paid sick days. A sign in the company lobby read "Happiness Headquarters." So. Much. Information. When does one expand? Cut back? Stop researching? When is enough enough? Like Colette's aging courtesan Lea in the *Chéri* books, I straddle two centuries that are drifting further and further apart. Will I, like Lea, quit scrambling for relevancy and simply give up? Or will I like Henry James, who straddled Victorianism and modernity, gain power from contradiction, from *too much*? All those commas and dashes; all those conditionals and misdirections; all those circumlocutions, erratic switches from intimacy to distance, heaps of ambiguous "it"s—in his late fiction, James' sentences simultaneously accrue and self-destruct as if composed with magic ink. There's too much punctuation, too much grammar—but just when we feel we cannot bear another twisted clause, the seduction of plot compels us onward. James' curvy syntax creates a centrifugal momentum that flings away dullness, spinning us into vortices of discovery and erasure, desire and loss. In *Dainty Desserts for Dainty People* (1915), Mrs. Knox, who was as far into her new century as I am into mine, wrote, "The pies and hot puddings of our grandmother's days have waned in popularity, and in their places are to be found cold and frozen desserts." By embracing gelatin's mutability, she forged a new era of sweets. "[Gelatin] may be used in an almost endless variety of ways. It makes possible numberless dishes, not less delightful to the eye than pleasing to the palate, and opens the door to constantly new achievements in culinary inventions." Like Henry James and

Mrs. Knox, am I advancing new paradigms? Or am I, as MFA fiction students often treat me, just weird?

When writing happens, my world shifts and like on *Marvel's Agents of Shield* a portal opens. Things tumble into it—events memories books movies the endless online garbage I read my body. The longer the portal is open, the more tumbles in. Patterns form, but on some level everything feels—everything *is*—connected so I keep pushing more and more stuff in. For each piece, I gather at least twice as much material as I need—and I buy talismans and souvenirs—snowflake obsidian pyramid, tiny bronze Steampunk rocket ship on a ball chain. Sorting through my notes is exhilarating and arduous. Sometimes I do multiple, progressively longer versions, piling paragraph upon paragraph, hoping that under all that weight startling connections will sprout. When do you close the portal? I don't know. While I'm in the thick of writing this essay, in fact, a male critic complains my pieces go on and on and on, and my confidence stumbles. I download Judy Grahn's 1974 lesbian-feminist anthem *A Woman is Talking to Death* and reread it. Regretting all the women she didn't love enough, didn't try to save, Grahn writes, "These are indecent acts, lacking courage, lacking a certain fire behind the eyes, which is the symbol, the raised fist, the sharing of resources, the resistance that tells death he will starve for lack of the fat of us, our extra." Defending our "fat," our "extra," we starve death. Grahn reminds me that for a woman, too much is always a form of resistance, and I regain momentum.

Collecting is about display. The curio cabinet my mother had for her blown glass clowns, the shelves a friend installed on his dining room wall to showcase his bounty of vintage vases. The vases are turquoise and sinuous, and even though I'm ignorant of their provenance I can tell from their presentation I should be impressed. Hoarding—even if others happen to see it—is never about display. My father's overloaded workroom in the basement, rows and rows of baby food jars filled with nuts and bolts and tiny nails—which begs the question—where did those jars come from? Was he amassing this stuff since I was an infant? Hoarding is a private act. You feel embarrassment and guilt over your manic accrual. The best writing embarrasses the author—at least a teeny bit—emerging from a compulsion to flaunt what any sane person would camouflage. The reader turns the page and witnesses the uncontainable—*panties around ankles*—and the energy that flares up astonishes. Work where the writer—or the workshop committee—is totally in control fails because its libidinal pressure has been critiqued away. The resultant piece is so polished, so correct, so flat you could bounce a dime off of it.

When my mother died, I started wearing one of her rings, a gaudy band encrusted with crushed diamonds. The week after her funeral, back in San Francisco I went for a Chi Nei Tsang treatment, a form of Taoist internal organ massage. My practitioner, Eréne, was a young woman who stood very erect. Her deep voice and her sternness combined with her excellent posture gave her the air of a cyborg. She occasionally worked with the dying, as a sort of doula, helping them cross over to the other side. So I was lying on my back on the massage table, and as soon as Eréne stepped up to me, she said, "Is that your mother's ring?" There was a shudder in her voice, as if she could feel death emanating from my finger. "You need to soak that in salt water to get rid of negative energy," she continued, "to allow only the good energy to remain." I didn't want to soak away anything, I wanted to cling to my mother's every last microbe. When Eréne would poke around my belly, I'd go into a trance and have visions. Eventually I'd come to with a huge gasp, just like in the movies. Even before she died, my visions were usually about my mother, as if I had these ancient memories stored in my colon, all the love and pain she and I shared for the fifty years that I knew her.

Nine out of every ten cells in my body is a colonizing microorganism. These communities of symbiotic bacteria and viruses and fungi that live on and inside my body are known as my microbiome, though I'm not sure "my" is appropriate here. As host, I contribute around 23,000 human genes, while microorganisms contribute over 9,000,000, which is a ratio of 390:1 human to microorganismal. Microorgasmic would be a livelier adjective, all these ecstatic mini-me's popping in and out of my anatomy. I've always suspected I wasn't an autonomous entity, but now there's scientific proof that this person known as Dodie is, in fact, a biomolecular network. I cannot be separated from my environment; I collect bits and pieces wherever I go. They adhere to me and change me. My physical being is a hoard. After my mother died, her empty house wasn't frightening, like I feared. I felt embraced as I walked from room to room, touching her things, absorbing her. I imagine those mother particles are still tumbling through me. Touching myself, I touch her.

I experience my psyche as similarly spongelike. Each gesture I make leaves a trail, happening within a vortex of communal gesture. Each step I take, my community steps with me. All the shit in my sociobiome, all its wonder, I can never shake off. No matter how othered I feel, I can never be other, not really. It is impossible to write about myself without writing my culture as well, for that culture infuses my personhood, even those aspects I despise. I consider America to be a shameful place—maybe it always has been—but right now much about this country is appalling. Fill in your own examples. If I pretend my writing can stand outside the shame that is America, that my ego-id-superego isn't driven by it, I'm not just lying to the reader, I'm lying to myself. In a recent trip to Los Angeles my plan was to drive directly from LAX to a gallery. I pulled into a mini-mall near the airport, starving and running late, and the only place to eat was HomeTown Buffet. Like how bad could it be? Atrocious, that's how bad. I choked down black-eyed peas with white rice, a few bites of ham, chicken, and salad. One cube of red Jell-O. Even the iced tea was inedible. Back in Indiana I used to go to a similar place with my mom for lunch—Old Country Buffet—when I was still a vegetarian—and I'd get a big salad and macaroni and cheese or some potato thing. And pudding and ice cream. So of course I felt pangs of her absence as I sat there among the overweight families, the old couples, single men. I was the only single woman in the place. I sat there alone—kids squealing with excitement over the desserts—picking at this toxic food. Station upon station of toxic food, and I could take as much as I wanted to—which makes this one of the most American places in the universe—and I thought of my chemo-riddled mother, her great pleasure at feeling well enough to leave the house and do something—anything—to please me—and I felt a loneliness so dense, it was as if the whole place was folding in on me, compacting. I felt sad and bland and utterly unspecial—and bummed that I hadn't eaten anywhere near $15 worth of food. It's a contest between you and the buffet, and in order to win you have to pile your plates high, like toppling high. *You say I can eat all I want—well, let me show you how much ALL can mean. I am the fucking champion of ALL.* Remembrance itself is a type of hoarding, a clutching at love or trauma—those "others" that make us fully human—and all of us are these futile Humpty Dumpties trying to put our shards back together again.

As I write this, my cat Quincey starts dying—more quickly—she's been terminally ill for years. She was my mother's cat, and she and

I grieved Mom together. In the eight years I've had her, I've done everything to keep Quincey alive. A $4,000 hospitalization, $200 acupuncture treatments. Life is precious. It is natural to try to keep it around as long as possible. The vet and I discuss her options, when to euthanize. What if she dies at home, I ask. He says I should wrap her body in a plastic bag and put it in the freezer—to keep it from oozing. Having a pet wrapped in plastic in the freezer—that's exactly the type of thing the worst hoarders do, the kind where cops/psychiatrists/distressed relatives cringe while crews wearing surgical masks or hazmat suits haul out their crap. In Los Angeles, Dennis Cooper lived next door to a code-red hoarder—Claire, an ancient white-haired woman. When Kevin and I slept on Dennis' sofa bed, Claire would peer in at us through the long strips of glass on either side of the front door. We happened to visit the weekend they cleared out her place. In my memory the event is totally silent. Workers carry out stuff, lumbering beneath their burdens like a line of ants hauling bread crumbs as Claire floats down the sidewalk, back and forth, totally untethered. There's not a sound in the air, not even the rustle of palm trees.

I read that I can alter my microbiome, make it more diverse, by spending time outdoors in dirt, by drinking kefir. I purchase kefir grains online and start fermenting. Kefir grains are thousands of years old. No one knows where they came from, and scientists have failed to synthesize them. The grains are said to be a gift from Allah. Some say they are bits of the original manna. Mine arrive dried, and I feed them organic raw milk. Slowly they reanimate, little mummies sucking up protein. As the grains awaken they look like small curds of cauliflower, like scrambled brains. I bought a white cotton cap for their mason jar, a circle of fabric edged with crocheted linen lace. Fastened to the jar with a red silicone band, the cap reminds me of Granny's bonnet the wolf put on in "Little Red Riding Hood." The kefir in its white bonnet is ravenous, requiring more milk each day. Its colonies of bacteria and yeast swell as it readies to enter, to better me. When I lift off the cap to shake the lumpy white liquid, I can feel its ancient presence and my body engorges. Soon I will meld with a time when God just reached down and handed us gifts.

I dream of Quincey. She's on the street staggering around, lost. I'm so glad to find her, as she's been missing for a long time. She's stumbling, one of her front legs injured, so I take her to the vet. The vet is very suspicious. I realize he's called Animal Control and he's taking Quincey away from me. I seize her and try to flee. I end up struggling with the vet. He's on top of me, choking me, and I'm struggling to breathe when I wake up. I wonder if the dream is about my guilt for having put her to sleep, for not defending the last dregs of her life—my fear that she's stumbling around in limbo. A gaunt ball of rumbling love—that was she. This daily energetic transaction. And then poof. No more energy. Like an appliance that's been unplugged. I write the dream in my journal with the awareness that I'd planned on working Quincey into the present essay, and the dream might fit in nicely. Quincey, my mother's cat, was an extension of my mother, the last living beat of her. My loss is infantile, a child on a rug shitting her pants and wailing maaaaaaaaaaaaahhhhhhhhhhhh. Yet here I am, caching it away for future use.

On Amazon, I purchase a set of Gigogne tumblers by Duralex— the six ounce size. At a party I was served wine in one, and a few days later, at a cafe, tea. I fell in love with them, their roundness. For the same reason—this roundness—I replaced my tube-shaped mugs with oversized teacups, breakfast cups—I lick their orbed contours and think of mother's milk. The Gigogne glasses, being heat resistant, are the most popular glasses in the Middle

East for drinking tea. I read that there is a photo of Osama Bin Laden holding one—but no matter how much I google Osama Bin Laden + Duralex, Osama Bin Laden drinking tea—I cannot find this image, which I have a passion to see. If I found it, I'm sure I'd save it to my hard drive like a treasured family snapshot. It's humiliating the way I hoard images information kitchenware food. What else—jewelry and clothes. I don't just buy a tin of a favorite tea, I order a whole pound. What else—pens and journals. I first heard of Duralex while translating a poem by Sabine Macher called "sur mon bureau." Even after five years of French in high school and college, my command of the language was so atrocious that my initial read of the title was "on my dresser." Rather than desk. The poem turned out to be a nightmare to translate—a list of objects with few subjects or verbs to contextualize them. Objects out of context, out of use value, become remarkably mysterious, wrapping their meaning tightly around themselves. Some Francophile explained to me what a Duralex "verre" was, and I put the full force of my obsessiveness behind coming up with an American equivalent. Nothing fit. We have Pyrex, but no brand of ubiquitous cheap glassware. So I left in Duralex as a spot of untranslatability—a site where language and culture stretch and waver—a wooziness that I reclaim in my curvaceous breast glasses. I lift one to my mouth and suck. Glass as tit. Dare/can I get that reductive here? I guess I am/can. In poetry workshops I was taught that separation from my mother—that painful wrenching apart—allowed my entry into the symbolic order—and thus language is about attempting to bridge this irrevocable gap—so that whenever I speak or write it is within a narrative of unbearable loss. I can only say "glass" if the glass and I are tragically separated. I can never fuse with the glass so I'm left with these stacks and stacks of words through which I try to pull the world towards me.

2

Leaky Boundaries

November 13–25, 2018—I give three readings/talks in London, one in Oxford, one in Berlin, and I deliver a paper at a Kathy Acker symposium in Karlsruhe. Throughout the trip devastating fires rage in Northern California, the Bay Area air quality going from unhealthy—red on the AirNow infographic—to very unhealthy—purple, and then brown, like a blood clot. I call my husband, and urge him to use the air filter; I log onto Amazon and order him an air mask for there are no air masks to be found in San Francisco. As in all disasters, you either prepare ahead of time or you are fucked.

No matter where we live, at home most of us feel underappreciated, maybe even lonely. In San Francisco I step out of a room where people shun me, avoiding eye contact. I fly 10 hours on a plane and enter another room where people hang on my every word, as if I had something important to say. Neither room feels right. Of course I prefer acceptance over disdain, but I'm leery of the performative public sphere. I've seen people addicted to it who become parodies of themselves, branded talking heads. There are so many rooms. My social worth goes up and down like a seismograph, and nothing seems real but blunt materiality. This chair. This podium. This smile thrust in my face. This quaking earth.

I'm spending my first night in London at the home of Paul Clinton, my former editor at *Frieze*, whom I've never met in person, but who lives in Lewisham, close to Goldsmiths where, on two hours of sleep, I'll be speaking that afternoon. Paul meets me at my train station, and instantly I adore him. He has a vivid conversational style in which it feels like he's leaping directly into your mind. He buys me a "flat white," a coffee drink no one can explain to me, but which seems to be a non-foamy cappuccino. My memory of the Goldsmiths reading is hallucinatory. There is an auditorium and students, and my host Simon Bedwell is taking my down coat and draping it over the front of the podium in order to block the giant Goldsmiths logo. Students ask probing questions I am incapable of answering.

It can be disconcerting reading for students, the way they stare at you passively, as if you were a TV. I'm used to reading to an audience of peers, where there is more of a feedback loop between you and them. I have mixed feelings about success. I want it, the recognition and any money that might come along with that, but marginality's cozy. There's little explaining—people either get you or ignore you. It always sounds exciting to be invited to the dinner after an opening, to be one of the in-crowd, to get free fancy food and unlimited booze until you find yourself in a room full of botoxed donors. Sometimes it's okay, sometimes you're seated next to a venture capitalist who might be venal but is lots of fun—or the husband of a curator who turns out to be an adventurer and who entertains you with a story of slaughtering a pig with a machete.

The next day I take the train to Oxford, a place that sucks, but I love the Ruskin School of Art, its students, the department's practice as research approach, the brilliant no-bullshit artist Corin Sworn who brought me here. One student I talk with is working with embroidery—she attaches fluffy substances onto stiff cloth with erratic red stitches; the result disturbing and a bit revolting as if Joseph Beuys had taken up the needle. Last year she had a breakdown/illness and this is how she passed her time, doing fucked up, irrational embroidery. For her it was a point of focus, both an endurance and a physical manifestation of destabilization. Turning a process so tight, so controlled, with its history of female compliance/usefulness—"busy hands are happy hands"—into an agent of chaos excites me.

Back in London, I stay with an old friend, artist Tariq Alvi, in his house in East Ham, a neighborhood teeming with Indian, Pakistani, and Eastern European immigrants—a respite from the mostly white entitlement of the rest of the trip. In London, person after person takes me aside and tells me they are working class. They say it privately, as if it were a sort of coming out, as if we were in a secret society. We share battle stories around fitting in, and bitch about the horrible elitism of the art world. Isabel Waidner, an organizer of the *This Reads Queer* event I take part in at the ICA, says her German accent helps her pass, but barely. We roll our eyes at Marxists who scoff at the working class, but what we hate most are those phony monsters who pretend to be working class, people whose parents are secretly attorneys or professors, and thus they have the social skills to spin some mileage out of the very thing that oppresses us.

In Berlin I stay in a condo with another old friend, Scott Watson, a Vancouver-based curator and art writer. My first night there he takes me to a birthday dinner for Krist Gruijthuijsen, director of the KW Institute for Contemporary Art, where I'll be reading in a couple days. The dinner is at a gallerist's home, an "urban oasis" that's received media attention due to its origins as a mid-20th-century gas station which the gallerist spent three years renovating. The second floor is a private gallery featuring his collection of George Grosz (1893–1959) drawings—biting satires of political and moral corruption. The Nazis hated him. Over thick veal chops, guests share stories of visits to a concentration camp where homosexuals were sent, and an East Berlin bunker where prisoners were psychologically tortured and then sold to West Berlin, so broken they could never assimilate back into society. Between courses I get up to use the toilet. The gallerist is in the kitchen performing his magic. He says the toilet is by the front door. I don't notice the four-inch step up to the foyer, and I trip and fall on my face. Splat. He helps me up, asks if I'm okay—I'm fine, I say—my arm hurts like hell—I'm fine, I whimper.

I return to the table, suppress my tears, and drink the gallerist's "*Pulp Fiction* wine." He consulted on the movie, and when Harvey Weinstein finally paid him, he spent the entire wad on an especially excellent vintage of Bordeaux. We're drinking the final few bottles. The *Pulp Fiction* wine is dry and austere, the opposite of the big jammy reds we brag about in California, the opposite of *Pulp Fiction* itself. The gallerist tells of a production meeting in which Harvey Weinstein threw an ashtray across the conference table. I find this comforting. Compared to Harvey Weinstein, my hurling into abjection across the gallerist's gleaming white floor is small potatoes.

Berlin doesn't let up, its history of trauma ever present. I feel like I'm walking through a gauntlet of spirits and I'm terrified of what they have to tell me. In the culture of object sex—people who have sexual relationships with objects—the Berlin Wall is very popular. Women fall in love with the Wall because it's so hated, misunderstood. They know the Wall was just trying to do a good job. It stood firm for 10,316 days, the scapegoat of a divided land. Women buy pieces of the Wall, make replicas of sections of it, which they masturbate with, in order to bond with and soothe the Wall. At the KW I read in the Pogo Bar, a creepy underground space, a rough-hewn cavern I'm told used to be a famous all-night dance club. It's airless and there's stone arches and I imagine sacrifices, blood splashed across corroded walls. I sit behind the mic and face the crowded, shadowy audience. I have a cold, my arm aches, my claustrophobia is buckling, and I give one of the best readings of my career.

I take the train to Karlsruhe, where I share a three-bedroom penthouse apartment above the Badischer Kunstverein with Matias Viegener and Leslie Dick. Though built in 1900, the arched metal front door looks ancient, and, of course, ominous. My first night there I dream of ghosts. In bed with me I feel a sort of rodent, plus an infant and a man and woman. When I manage to get up I see a guinea pig ghost scurrying down the hall. I see a woman with a baby and a youngish guy with dark hair. They are malevolent. I try to use my energy field to block the man's intimidating energy, but he is too powerful for me. So, later I'm awake and in the kitchen making coffee and reporting all this to Matias and Leslie. When the guinea pig ghost comes up, Leslie says in amazement that a favorite student at CalArts makes paintings of the ghost of his guinea pig! So now I don't know if I really met some ghosts or if I hooked into Leslie's leaky subconscious.

Taking no chances, I buy white sage at the health food store, and in the evening I smudge my room, clearing it of unwelcome forces. And then I go hang out in the kitchen to deconstruct the first day of the Kathy Acker Symposium with Matias. When I return to my room the door's slammed shut, and I'm unable to open it. "Matias," I'm yelling, "help me with this!" We get the door open, and Matias says it was just a breeze. I say that I haven't closed the door at all because it's so difficult, you have to push your whole weight against it. Matias: "It's an old building, it was a breeze." Me: "I sage it and then it slams shut—come on!" Matias says, "Honey if you get scared in the night, you can crawl in bed with me." The sage must have worked—for the next three nights I see no ghosts and only have pleasant dreams.

The Kathy Acker Symposium, like all conferences, is a mélange of narcissism, rigor, and tenderness. I learn more about Kathy Acker than I ever dreamed of knowing. When I tell artist Kaucyila Brooke that I feel guilty for eating veal in Berlin, she says that the veal in Germany tends not to be milk-fed, so you're not eating tortured baby cow—just dead baby cow. And this gives me comfort.

3

The Violence of the Image

Last month the 1959 low-budget monster movie *Behemoth* was on TV. I watched just the ending. The Behemoth, which looks like an elongated dinosaur with bulgy eyes, wiggles mechanically through the ocean. It's way bigger than the submarine that's trying to destroy it. Wham! It bashes against the side of the sub and water starts leaking from an overhead pipe, provoking tense meaningful eye contact between the two officers manning the controls. They maneuver for a better aim. One yells, "Fire!" and the other grits his teeth and presses a plunger, unloading a bomb that hits the monster in the head. It thrashes and sinks. "That's it?" I thought. "They killed the thing with one shot?" These days it would take at least 15 minutes of fast-cut struggle, for we citizens of the 21st century have learned that evil does not die easily. No longer is evil focused like a bad tooth you can root out and get on with your good life. Increasingly diffuse, the Big Scary now spreads across networks, sprouting anywhere. We have global warming; we have public executions that shock without warning; we have toxic waters, honey bees threatened with extinction, warnings of plague. In the White House Americans have installed an irrational, lying, unaccountable crook who rages against "radical Islamic terrorists," an embarrassingly redundant term. Isn't radical implied in terrorist? Have you ever heard of a middlebrow terrorist? A centrist terrorist? A give-a-cop-a-can-of-Pepsi-and-heal-the-world terrorist? When you're an American, you've got so much to be embarrassed about. The US has become a very stupid country, and stupidity married to power is danger squared. We've given a buffoon the nuclear codes.

To be radical you need a wall to bounce your radicalism off of. When you live in a soup of cover ups, corruption and general smarminess, is it possible to clear the mire enough to even find that wall? Those on the radical left claim—and rightly so—that global capitalism is the enemy. But late capitalism is a slippery beast, able to incorporate just about anything into its ravenous maw and spit it back out with a price tag attached. Blind, profit-driven virulence has infiltrated everything, its poison creeping both inside and outside of us. The Behemoth has swallowed the submarine and here we are, flailing in the slimy dark. In another 1950s cult favorite, *The Wild One*, a dancing blonde asks biker Marlon Brando, "Hey, Johnny, what are you rebelling against?" He bongos the top of a jukebox and snarls, "Whatta ya got?" What do we "got"? That is the central question facing us today. Without a focus, without a specific monster in mind to boom boom boom, radical enthusiasm can grind down to depression. We stop reading the news; we post pix of cats on Facebook, flowers on Instagram, obsessively checking for likes. Or, like overcrowded rodents, we attack one another.

I've got a stalker. I used to be her favorite writer, but when I posted bad opinions in the comments box of another poet's Facebook thread, her admiration switched to disdain. She instantly hated me and all I stood for, even things I didn't realize I stood for, and she began an assault across social media, ridiculing and accusing me. I find it difficult, today, to forgive the poets who left encouraging comments for her. I felt shunned and despised, like there was no love in the world for me. Presently emails from online shopping sites began appearing in my inbox, confirming orders I didn't order, informing me my credit card had been declined. My stalker is a monster. She wouldn't argue with this. Making herself into a monster makes her feel special. It is difficult for the entitled to feel special. Tattoos and heavy eyeliner and revealing little dresses—everybody—even fat girls—has those. She posts pictures of her ass to social media; she likes pastries and favors the word "super." My stalker is a bully. A bully can smell someone who has been previously bullied—the bully and the bullied fit together like jigsaw puzzle pieces. I imagine her alone in the middle of the night, ashtray on her nightstand overflowing with butts, drunk, or buzzed on Adderall, maybe both, afraid to sleep due to last night's bout of sleep paralysis, the tension is unbearable—tight jaw compacted heart—she searches for something crappy online—adds it to her shopping cart, enters my name address phone number, which she copied down the summer she interned for that radical indie press—her taut little body vibrates as she enters a fake credit card number, presses the PLACE ORDER button, pummeling me with hubcaps peonies guitar strings silk sock liners—what a fucking rush what a release—almost as good as the burst she gets when she slices her inner thigh with a razor blade—it's like she's sending me all her pain, her disappointment her god-awful ordinariness. Afterwards she feels a terrible intimacy, that of the torturer who comes to love her victim.

With the election of Trump, poets decided that the only acceptable way to depict an American flag was upside down. When a provocateur poet posted a flag rightside up on Instagram, there was an angry Facebook thread about it. Poet A said that if he had known the flag poet was so fucked up, he never would have had him read in his series. Poets B and C proposed informing the flag poet's employer about the offense and getting him fired. None of the poets noticed that the posted flag wasn't a real American flag, but the fake Chinese-made flag that had been in the news, the one that unwitting patriots had purchased, with too many stars. Kevin back-channeled poet B and pointed this out: *That is not the regular flag. It has far too many stars. It is the 61-star flag that indicates the alternate history of America. Whether or not that's a good thing or a bad depends how you feel about the flag today, and if you believe that the US took a wrong turn somewhere back in history. The regular flag has only 50 stars— supposedly for each state in the union.* However, poet B didn't back down. He said he couldn't understand what a 61-star flag would signify. He said that regardless of the flag poet's intention, to be oblique on something this sensitive was aggressive, and the ride-side-up flag still reinscribed violence. If one is vague, poets will project the worst into your words. If you refer to a person but don't name names, poets will assume it's themselves or someone you'd never dream of. At Alley Cat Books the reader launches into a poem so politically correct you could bounce a dime off of it, political in all the right ways—and a poet in the audience starts nodding his head wildly back and forth as if it were a rattle. The rest of the reading he has a normal head. Political writing is straightforward, plain, and "learned," prefaced by a declaration of the author's identity markers. *As a white cis American working class college-educated Baby Boomer who lives in California and prefers unoaked Chardonnay . . . .* Political writing is careful about who owns what experience. Someone tweets: *She doesn't have the right to talk about that*, and you feel shame. When a poet rants against me and the politics of my writing on Facebook, she begins with "What kind of woman would . . . ." *What kind of woman* implies a correct, proper version of femaleness—and I—not being that kind of woman—have crossed over into an impossible otherness. It doesn't matter what else she goes on to accuse me of, *What kind of woman* has declared me an abomination. Since childhood I've been criticized for my nonstandard female embodiment. I was savage and unruly, clomping through life like a bull—and now I'm an old white feminist—an oppressor in a pink pussy hat. The Facebook poet's curses scatter across my features like the points in facial recognition software, a surveillance grid that hardens on my face like a mask. No expression is possible in the tightness of her projections. Thought criminals need to be rooted out and shunned, the dead as well as the living. Cindy Sherman. Gandhi. Marjorie Perloff. Walt Whitman. *And what I assume you shall assume, / For every atom belonging to me as good belongs to you.* Community walks within me and thus I contain both criminal and accuser. The idiocy of the American government, I contain that as well. In a muck of warring poets, I spew that war. Heriberto Yépez: *Networks are both migrants and the gatekeepers.* The madness of social media, it too walks within me. I operate in the dangerous and contradictory realm of the in-between. Neither goddess nor heroine, I am an old white feminist, a shriveled hag envious of my stalker's fertility and youthful beauty. My hair is coarse and unkempt; my long hanging dugs bounce about like phalluses. I befoul Poetry with my personal essays, which are riddled with superstition, deceit, defective intelligence, lust, and debauchery. I am simultaneously horrific and ridiculous. My politics are so odious I've made pacts with rapists. Though he's taken the form of a goat, I kiss the abuser's backside; I apologize for him.

In a skit called "Silver Surfers," Tracey Ullman plays a teacher who shows seniors how to troll the internet. A woman says she'd like to see her grandson's YouTube channel. Tracey turns on a video of a grade school boy demonstrating something. She notes

Stuff My Stalker Has Ordered for Me Online

1. 1961 DODGE POLARA HUBCAP - 15" WHEEL COVER
2. BLISS FUZZ' OFF™ BIKINI PRECISION HAIR REMOVAL CREAM/2 OZ - 2 TUBES
3. SUPER-SENSITIVE SUPREME CELLO STRING SET - 4/4 SIZE
4. GE DRYER FLAT STYLE IGNITOR - PART #: WE4X750
5. CUSTOM CHROME FINISH 13-INCH HUBCAP
6. CAMERA KALEIDOSCOPE 4"WX2"DX3"H - QTY 4
7. KINGSTON PASTEL TUFTED CHENILLE BEDSPREAD BLUE - CALIFORNIA KING
8. DUNLOP D404 110/90-18 FRONT TIRE
9. FOREST FRIENDS ORNAMENTS FELT KIT - QTY 3
10. FRUIT OF THE LOOM LITTLE GIRLS' TODDLER 6 BRIEFS/ASSORTED/SIZE 4T - QTY 4
11. COLLAPSIBLE FILE BOXES, WITH CHROME HANDLES, LETTER SIZE, 4 PER CARTON - QTY 2
12. GEORGETTE FLORAL DRESS/SAGE FLORAL - SIZE: 10 PETITE - QTY 2
13. HOLD MY HEART PERIDOT STAINLESS STEEL CREMATION JEWELRY - QTY 2
14. SAMSUNG BD-H6500 - SMART BLU-RAY PLAYER WITH 4K UP-SCALE WIFI 3D - OPEN BOX
15. IRIS SIBIRICA KITA-NO-SEIZA - PACK OF 3 BULBS
16. DIANE VON FURSTENBERG SILK PETAL-PRINT A-LINE DRESS, FLORAL CHECK ROSE - SIZE 10
17. LITE USE COMPUTER TASK CHAIR WITH ARMS AND DRAFTING KIT - BLACK
18. KINGSIZE HOSTA - 1 BULB
19. NIKON COOLPIX AW130 WATERPROOF SHOCKPROOF FREEZEPROOF DIGITAL CAMERA 8GB BUNDLE - YELLOW
20. BROWNELLS MOLY BORE TREATMENT PASTE - 2 OZ - 3 JARS
21. PEONY WHITE CAP - 2 BULBS
22. TETRA POND AQUASAFE TAP WATER CONDITIONER - 2 101.4-OZ BOTTLES
23. THREE ASSEMBLED MINIATURE WIDOW'S WALK RAILS
24. DERM EXCLUSIVE 30-DAY 4-PIECE INTRODUCTORY COLLECTION WITH FILL AND FREEZE BONUS
25. UNISEX MID-CALF SOCK LINERS IN WASHABLE SILK/CREAM/SIZE M - 5 PAIRS

how the video is amateurish in quality, and tells the class that when you see somebody getting it wrong online it's important to point it out to them. Tracey instructs the class to click the thumbs down button—or if they want to make it more personal to post a comment, using a fake name, in which they say either he has a voice like a girl or everyone here wishes he were dead. Tracey types on the grandmother's computer, "Wish you were dead, loser." "It's a real thrill when you click that send button," she says.

The internet, like late capitalism, is everywhere and nowhere. My stalker sends me objects that are not objects. They're images I keep trying to push into language. According to capitalism, what you own you are. Lawn plants, chenille bedspread, frilly dresses, Forest Friends felt Christmas ornament kit, fish pond water conditioner, hubcaps. What is the stalker saying to/about me through these suburban talismans? According to capitalism, whoever controls images controls the world. I say to my psychic, I think I know who's been stalking me, but I'm not sure. My psychic says, *you know*. How can I control these images that have been thrust upon me? I imagine a woman who wears floral dresses, a widow with a four-year old toddler. She loved her husband and always wears a peridot pendant that contains a bit of his ashes. She's a photographer who plays the cello and drives a motorcycle. Alone in the house she feels vulnerable, so she keeps a gun under her pillow. She has a home office, a file box where she stores her photos. She's femmy and a bit old fashioned. She sleeps under a tufted chenille bedspread; she uses face firming creams and bikini exfoliators. She's trying to fix herself up to get another man. She gardens, preferring bulb plants from Holland—so she lives somewhere with a yard, a rural or suburban landscape. People do not suspect her wildness—the gun, the motorcycle—but it's there waiting to take over. She likes bargains, preferring to buy things on sale, with coupon codes or open boxes. She has a Blu-ray player to help her through her lonely nights. Or maybe she met a man who owns a gun. He's a rebel who deserves her bikini-groomed snatch. This new man likes porn; when she's ready he plans to share some with her on the Samsung Blu-ray player he noticed in the living room. They sit in her garden with its lush greens, irises and peonies, holding hands, kissing lightly, then more and more passionately. Let's make it the guy who has the motorcycle. He's a Marlon Brando type—a vet who's living off of disability—going to art school in photography, and these things my stalker ordered are gifts for him, the wheel, the gun cleaner, the camera. She drives a car—a fully restored '61 Dodge Polara, which totally impresses the vet. That's how they met—at a light he pulled up beside her on his motorcycle and asked her if she wanted to grab some coffee. After the coffee, the woman and the photographer fuck in the garden beside the koi pond, which is mercifully devoid of chlorine fumes thanks to Tetra Pond AquaSafe Tap Water Conditioner. Their sex is protected from nosey neighbors by a clump of kingsize hostas. The female koi are named after female science fiction writers, Doris Lessing, Octavia Butler; the male fish are named after 20th century avant-garde composers, Boulez, Webern. Last week raccoons ate Ursula K. Le Guin, and before that they got Joanna Russ and Schoenberg, so that the woman is considering replacing the koi with a cheaper species, such as goldfish. The vet's cock is pink and clean, squeaky clean like the Army taught him to keep it in their anti-VD training videos, well-scrubbed as his gun, the barrel of which he regularly plunges with Brownells Moly Bore Treatment Paste. The woman's Diane von Furstenberg dress is pushed up to her waist. The vet pulls out his Nikon Coolpix and shoots a close up of the twig and gravel scratches on her ass. The Samsung Blu-ray player blasts "Bang a Gong." HUBCAP DIAMOND STAR HALO. According to capitalism, accessories are personality. Commodities morph into character traits, morph into narrative momentum. Personal memories and product reviews on Amazon provide supplemental details. My fuck scene would be more erotic if there were more of a buildup but the woman is always ready. Too eager, perhaps. She can come without touching herself. Her cunt is so strong it could lift barbells, if she owned any. Sometimes the photographer complains she's clenching him too tightly, but her cunt is ravenous for him, wants to absorb every drop his cock can offer. Afterwards she doesn't wash, enjoying his semen smeared over her legs and belly, dripping out of her, and besides, the stalker hasn't ordered her any soap.

The first target of massive internet shaming and harassment was Monica Lewinsky, in 1998. She was 22 years old and, being the first, she had no context or support to help her cope. These days she finds comfort and purpose in her work with anti-harassment and bullying organizations. Her taped phone conversations with Linda Tripp are available on YouTube, hours of rambling female intimacy. I envy the closeness of the two women, the way they coddle the micro details of one another's lives—everything from the temptation of donuts at the hairdresser—Monica's favorite is white frosting with multi-colored sprinkles—to why won't Bill call me. The conversations begin after Clinton has dumped Monica and track her heartbreak and desperate attempts to contact him. I'd love to have a girlfriend I could talk to endlessly about all my shit—someone as doting and supportive as Linda, someone who would slather me with such love. The betrayal by Tripp alone would devastate anyone—and that's just a footnote to Monica's collapse. If old feminists ruled the world, one woman defiling another would be a capital offense.

On Facebook, a male poet posts a photo of a naked man striding down the street. In the comments section, a female poet writes she finds the photo so upsetting her hands are shaking, and she just has to speak out. She's decided the person in the photo is a mentally ill homeless man—even though there is nothing in the photo or the male poet's post that announces that. Her extreme reaction to her (own) invented narrative prompts her to condemn the male poet and the hundred people who liked the image. I read on the internet that suggesting self-control online is *tone policing*, and I am wrong to go there. Maybe she's right, we're all a bunch of assholes laughing at the disenfranchised—or maybe he's a gay nudist—in San Francisco it's not uncommon to see naked men walking down the street, alone or in groups. The photo is of the man's back, taken at a distance, maybe he has a glittering gold tube sock stuck on his cock. I've seen so many men with socks on their cocks—including panhandling teens on Castro Street. To get more money, I assume. No matter how much you stare at the image, it refuses to cough up more clues. Is it possible to keep your righteous fingers away from the keyboard? Is it possible to live without diminishing or oppressing another? Jain ascetics with soft brooms made of shed peacock feathers, gently sweeping the ground lest they step on an insect. What are the limits of reverence?

We make soup, we write tight little narratives where all messy threads are tied up, neatly, at the end. We read books on organizing our home. Rooms turn vast with order, with simplicity. We have only what we need, what we cherish, and there is a place for everything we own. Possessions are instantly findable and they are happy to serve us. The stalker destroys time, categories and meaning, locking memories and dreams in the present moment. The mind strains against the body to push thoughts out. Everything is impure. The daily taunts and jeers I experienced as a child are happening right now right here. I'm pooping my guts out, taking slow breaths against the pain. My body is twisting my subjectivity, wringing it out like one of those old-time washing machines my grandmother had. Whenever anyone laughs they are laughing at me. The stalker has broken the frame. The process of writing this essay creates a new frame that proves I am capable of at least the most basic adult human functioning. How do you express trauma when linearity fails you? You order products online for your enemy. When the past possesses the present you enter the now now now of spurting adrenaline, and your irises spin like pinwheels. The pix shriek nobody wants you here the pix shriek you are hated everybody hates you. I publish a piece in a journal my stalker has also published in. I imagine her reading it with scorn, searching for bits out of context she can use to destroy me. "Dodie Bellamy said" becomes a tagline to ruin. On *Nashville*, Will, the gay character, is being bashed on Twitter and bam! his trauma is my trauma panic blots out the present like one of those bags terrorists shove over a captive's head. I am forever a child useless and humiliated. I am a radiant pink clit inflamed by the eros of my stalker's loathing.

My stalker hates capitalism. I believe she hates capitalism more than she hates me. Headline on the internet: *A majority of millennials now reject capitalism, poll shows*. My stalker says that if she could have anything in the world she wished for, it would be to destroy capitalism. My stalker believes that by shoplifting items made by slaves in China she is fucking capitalism. When I was young I'd shoplift with friends but I was too much of a pussy to do it on my own. My friend Jackie—who was a pro—and I would come home with huge hauls of stuff, most of which I'd end up not wanting, and I had to figure out how to get rid of. Before we went on a run, we'd put on makeup and work dresses and little heels; our aesthetic was *clueless middle class bargain hunter*. Jackie's first rule: no backpacks or large purses while shoplifting. We carried moderately-sized shoulder bags. They looked like they couldn't hold much of anything—but you'd be surprised. I once smashed a fluffy pink prom dress into one. Jackie's second rule was entitlement. When she found a stainless steel fish poacher she liked, she just picked it up and marched out of Macys with it, and nobody blinked. Despite its heart-thumping arousal, hours of nonstop shoplifting was exhausting. I felt buried in commodity culture and the treadmill of consumption that drives capitalism's insatiable thrust. It was gross. When Jackie and I returned to my apartment, we dumped our haul onto my bed in a jumbled mountain, and then we belly-flopped onto it, shrieking, carefree as dogs rolling around in shit.

One night, over a period of two hours, thirteen things were ordered in my name, each from a different website. Then a couple of hours later, another item, bringing the total to fourteen in one evening. Could one person possibly have ordered this much, this quickly? Or was somebody throwing a Harass Dodie party? I sat down at my desk and started emailing the companies—This order is fraudulent. I also downloaded the product photos per artist friend Kristina Lee Podesva's suggestion. When I told her about my stalker, excitement spread across Kristina's face and she exclaimed, "Document this!" The order confirmations were coming in so furiously I couldn't keep up. I could only imagine that the person on the other end was tweaking. I checked my stalker's Twitter feed. She tweeted before the ordering frenzy began and then not again until ten or fifteen minutes after it ended, when she wrote—My mother just asked me if I was on heroin. A few minutes later she tweeted—I'm reading in Philadelphia, if you come bring me flowers—peonies. Peony bulbs were one of the fourteen items. The world goes crazy with connection. I say to my psychic, I think I know who it is, but I'm not sure. My psychic says, *you know*. My stalker sends me a widow's walk and a necklace to contain the ashes of a loved one—is she casting a spell of doom on me? What does an office chair mean? It requires work for me to write back to all these companies, but it also requires a hell of a lot of commitment and focused attention for her to order all this stuff. Her curated images are about potential, about our post-industrial condition, in which we sit at machines pushing around bytes, alone, longing to reach out. Glamor shots of merchandise hail her and she clicks them with the grammarless fever of a rat clicking a food-delivery lever. Eventually the image objects arrive on my computer and I click them with confusion and fear and anger, but also with a twinge of pleasure that reminds me of playing *Monument Valley*, my bumbling attempts to navigate a twisting architecture whose rules endlessly elude. Objects speak with the indeterminacy of a cry, garbled like puppets with their lips sewn shut. Yet it's impossible not to narrativize them. To the protest, my stalker wears cotton toddler panties stretched tight across her cooch. Beneath her sheer Diane Von Furstenberg dress, areolas bloom, lush pink peonies. Comrades and government infiltrators alike find her unbearably sexy. Anything you send a writer is a gift. A suicidal young woman pulls up on a motorcycle. I rub her face into my desiccated crotch, suck the bloom from her cheeks and cough up bile. My breath is so foul sperm curdles and young Marxists faint. *I too am not a bit tamed, I too am untranslatable,/ I sound my barbaric yawp over the roofs of the world.*

Before I became a middle class person I shopped only at thrift stores, so the clothes I owned were jeans, striped long-sleeved tees, and party dresses. When I got my first middle class job, I went to Macys and charged these awful outfits—polyester pants suits, etc.—I looked like a clown, a droopy professional clown. The middle class likes different things than the working class, but we all want things things things things—even homeless people in my neighborhood wheel shopping carts and suitcases overflowing with things. If capitalism were destroyed, would the homeless have better things? The viscosity of capitalism swallows us. We are never sure if we are inside or outside of it. It spreads over the globe making things stick together. I walk down the street wearing bits of China India Portugal Vietnam, and occasionally the USA. The ghosts of nameless workers vape from my silhouette, rendering me not one but many. My boss said my best middle class outfit was one I shoplifted with Jackie—a navy cashmere shift by Ralph Lauren. For the bourgeois subject wouldn't guilt be a more appropriate response than hate? Perhaps guilt is what's really behind the attacking of those perceived politically impure. Like a game of tag, you spread the cooties to those not deft enough to sidestep your fingering. Anyone who's seen a zombie movie knows that when capitalism is destroyed we don't get utopia. We get poetry bandits who police the perimeters. Law like a person has an unconscious. What my stalker really wants to destroy is the stink of trauma that wafts off of her.

I provide a focal point for my stalker's hate, a manageable target for the all-consuming vastness of her rage. If she didn't have me, maybe she'd jump off a bridge or shoot up a post office, who knows. It's the middle of the night and all this pressure is trapped in her body, enormous pressure she can't release. She wants to sigh, to scream, to burst out crying. But nothing moves. Stuck in a limbo of angst, where sadness and fury are all mucked up together, ongoing and escalating, my stalker looks over her list of enemies. It's Dodie tonight. People rarely do things just to be wicked—they act because they're convinced they've encountered evil, convinced that innocents need protecting—or they perceive their livelihood is threatened—or a great wrong has been committed against them. Throughout history, horrible things—I don't need to list them—have been done with God on our side, things that must have felt honorable at the time, but whose cruelty today shocks us. Powerful feelings can fuck you up, especially when fucked-up you feel you have the right to fuck up others. On the internet I read about a guy who stalked a woman for five years. Helen reported 125 incidents of harassment but the police did nothing until he attacked her with a pair of scissors, stabbing her multiple times on the neck, face, and back. It took a lot of googling to find out what Helen did to deserve her "living nightmare." She met Joseph at a halfway house where she was recovering from an eating disorder. They became friends, until one night Joseph asked Helen to drive him and another friend to see a band called Carnaby Street. Helen didn't feel up to it and said she'd text him if she changed her mind. Joseph felt stood up, and his affection for Helen instantly turned into burning hatred. So he vandalized her car, made silent phone calls, left a dead cat on her doorstep, smashed her windows, sent her letters calling her fat and rat-faced, spray-painted Die Helen across a brick wall, nearly killed her. Because she didn't go to a concert. There is always a reason to destroy another. Anybody who needs a reason will find one. I was my stalker's favorite writer until I posted a comment on a poet's Facebook thread, three years ago. Before that I have no memory of having met her or heard of her. Though I think that's not true; most likely I was in many rooms with her, rooms filled with poetry.

I learn from the internet that mobbing should not be confused with gang stalking. Mobbing is perpetrated by a closed, defined group, such as an academic department or poetry community. Gang stalking is perpetrated by government/corporate agencies. Black vans sit outside your apartment, trail you down the street. Satellites beam voices into your brain via nanotechnology implanted in your skull. The voices are relentless and abrasive. They say everybody hates you. They urge you to harm yourself and others. Eventually you find out you are part of a vast government/corporate experiment whose goal is to break people, and then through mind control to create spies who don't even know they're spies. Mind control makes the best kind of spy because no matter how much the targeted individual is tortured, they can't reveal secrets they don't know they have. Their secrets are hidden deep within their brain behind an altar that only the programmers know how to unlock. The Russians have implanted nanotechnology inside Trump's head, and that's why he does their bidding. The programmers can kill you by remote control, make your heart clench, make you vomit liters of black goo. The whole thing's set up to look like paranoid schizophrenia so that targeted individuals aren't taken seriously. But these people hold conventions and tell their stories to the masses via websites and YouTube videos. *Vice* made a documentary about them. The psychological torture is so intense, many targeted individuals commit suicide. Some of them give in to the voices and go on a shooting spree. The internet is a cacophony of voices beaming love or hate at you, depending on your age race gender sexual preference body type politics. The internet can gather 2000 signatures against you overnight. You can be condemned on the merest wisp of data. Even if you aren't the one who committed a crime, if you criticize mob action in the comment section of a poet's Facebook feed, you're labeled an apologist and you're just as evil as the worst rapist or racist, and young women you barely know will hate you forever. If you protest they'll hate you even more. If you block them on Facebook they'll condemn you for silencing them. They'll post screenshots of things you've written—out of context—and since you're old and not as online savvy you don't know how to make each post discrete, like a hologram with its context imbedded within it rather than depending on other posts for context. Powerful male mentors will boost their slanderous lies about you and no one will come to your defense except Brian Kim Stefans, who lives like a million miles away in Los Angeles. Locals will tell you privately they agree with you and they're appalled by your treatment but they dare not say anything. And young guys who you thought were your friends will lecture you on your anti-feminist behavior. There's only one response available to any guy who would lecture you on feminism and that's fuck off, but still your heart breaks because you cared for them in an age-appropriate way, as if they were cute spaniels with big floppy ears. The poetry community you've been devoted to since the early '80s is no longer safe, and even those who didn't mob you, you see them mobbing others, and this you cannot abide. On the internet you learn that when someone is directing negative energy at you, you should imagine yourself covered by mirrors and bounce that negative energy back to them. You should ground yourself by drinking chlorophyll, trace minerals, and specially ionized water.

By harassing me does my stalker believe she's saving Poetry or is she merely a sociopath lusting for blood? I read on the internet that stalking is like a long rape. Before such violence there is no place for obliqueness. Every piece I've ever written has centered around love, no matter how fucked up its manifestation. But this girl and her actions, I can find no love here to cling to, not even a spark. She's like that evil queen who fed Snow White the poison apple. She's a cliché of viciousness the internet has birthed. I sit at the computer fortressed in mirrors, my eyes peering through a narrow slit. I click the Mail icon. Something new has been ordered—three jars of moly bore treatment paste. I learn on the internet that you rub this paste on the inside of your rifle barrel in order to reduce friction for minimum fouling, faster, easier cleanup and longer barrel life. My stalker posts Tinder screenshots from interested guys below her league and ridicules them. She posts provocative pictures of herself—flimsy teddies and wisps of panties she can pull aside in order to selfie her ass—and fantasizes the FBI agents she's sure are surveilling her because she's a radical are jerking off to her image. When I was a child I fantasized God was watching me, and so I would do cute things for God, inspired by the TV show *Candid Camera*, which made Cold War surveillance culture fun. At any moment you could step out of ordinary life and do something adorable or amusing enough to be broadcast to all of America. With earbud attached to a coiled cord that trails from ear to back of neck and disappears into their dark jackets, FBI agents are forced to observe you. It is their job to remain professional and implacable, but your dirty talk on Twitter, your skimpy selfies are so damned seductive—flies zip open, well-scrubbed cocks pop out, sunglassed heads arc backwards in rapture. I learn on the internet that people who try to harm you are in fact possessed by negative entities, entities that they are unaware of. Therefore I say to my stalker—*You need to ground and clear yourself because you seem to be possessed. In your latest selfies you look awfully animalistic. You should drink some chlorophyll and wear a lead-lined hoodie to bed to protect yourself from the government/corporate complex that is beaming these terrible thoughts into your head.*

4

The Pink Place

Aimee Goguen creates claustrophobic sexual landscapes which viewers can project onto but which create too much discomfort for them to ever fully enter. Thus watching Goguen's videos is profoundly moving. In *Tongue Job* two tightly framed guys French kiss for three minutes and forty seconds. One guy is lying on his back, as the other looms over, holding the supine guy's chin and head. It's not a gentle hold, more like a clamp, but not hostile either. The horizontal guy seems passive, and the top guy guzzles his tongue like a starving dog.

For the first half of the video, the screen rolls, and bands of static occlude the image. The sex act, which you're so eager to observe, degrades into abstraction. Instead of turning you on, the rolling screen induces vertigo. You want to walk over and bang the screen as if it were a crappy rabbit-eared TV with bad reception. Halfway through, when the rolling and visual static cease, and we finally get a good look at what's happening, Goguen amps up the sound static, which at least for this overly-sensitive viewer, both irritated me and put me on edge, mucking with my ability to maintain what philosopher Julia Kristeva termed my "clean and proper" self. There's a gleefulness in Goguen's repeated disruption of pleasure. You either watch these sloppy kissers on her terms or you don't watch them at all—which reminds me of advice my mentor Bruce Boone gave me back in the '80s: "Writing is an SM relationship between the writer and the reader, and, you, Dodie, as writer, need to learn to be the top." Never once do you get so caught up in the sex you forget you're watching a video. Goguen's mark-making is incessant.

On her blog, beneath a still from *Tongue Job*, Goguen writes, "This boy ate at the pink place." As we enter the ferocious pink place, our desire to be consumed, which is so hot, wars with terror at dissolution, which nauseates. As in all good sex, we lose control of our reactions—they rage and sputter, returning us to our animal essence. The slurped tongue looks unprotected, shell-less as a slug. (On her blog page for this video, "slug" is one of the tags Goguen assigns to the post.) I'm reminded of Megan Milks' fantasy "Slug," in which a woman has wild sex with a giant gastropod. "Slug kisses Patty. Slug kisses Patty until Patty can't breathe. Slug is in her nostrils and in her mouth. Slug's mucus drips down her throat and fills her lungs. Slug's mucus fills her body." In Milks' story, Slug is a muscular powerhouse, but here the slug-tongue is obscenely vulnerable, an organ so aroused it's lost its drive for self-preservation. A brainless pink undulating sucked thing. How long can it maintain its blobby integrity before it splits open and disintegrates?

Holding supine guy's head and jaw, ravaging his tongue, top guy seems to be operating him like a puppet. Goguen complicates their relationship in a brief interlude where we just see passive guy's head. He sticks out his insanely long tongue and flails it against a periwinkle blue background. This is the one moment in the video that seems directed. It's an interlude, a lashing dance announcing the triumph of agency. Then the top guy swoops down, clamps on his mouth and the frenetic pink visuals continue. The periwinkle backdrop was actually the lover's T-shirt; in our deranged state his T-shirt is vast enough to fill the frame/the room/the world. Besides being a shade of blue, a periwinkle is also a marine snail said to be meaty like a clam and sweet like an oyster. *To eat a periwinkle, you must bring the opening of the shell to your lips and suck: not too forcefully like a vacuum but not too gently, either.* Despite his vampiric enthusiasm, who knows what's going on inside the mouth of periwinkle guy as he goes down on bottom guy's siren tongue. Perhaps it is he who is being drained from the inside out.

In the pink place we all love a good bout of annihilation. Bobbing nose. Chin stubble harsh against slinky molluskan mouths. Distended flesh fillet convulsing in and out of abstraction, pink mouth pink slug fur-bristle. No longer than a rock video, *Tongue Job*'s three minutes and forty seconds feel like an unendurable expanse, a headfuck that entices and revolts. Bottom guy's mouth is stretched wide like they're always telling me to do at the dentist's. It's not easy to maintain—neither is sticking out your tongue from the root and holding it there. What's active? What's passive? Who is subject who is object who is top/bottom who owns the periwinkle? During the final few moments of the video, the camera pans to the eyes and nose of the supine one. All we see of the puppeteer is his fingers and a patch of blue tee. Though supine guy fills the screen, he seems elsewhere. His head jiggles, but of whose accord? We have no access to him. His eyes are closed and his lashes are very long.

5

The Endangered Unruly

I became interested in Mary Beth Edelson for self-centered reasons. I read that she was born and raised in East Chicago, Indiana, a mere six miles from Hammond, my hometown. Edelson has described East Chicago as a "booming multi-racial steel mill town of immigrants." My brother worked in the steel mill she's referencing. Rust Belt Indiana is a place nobody comes from, and nothing interesting ever happens there. But Mary Beth Edelson came from there, so I have an urge to see her as a spiritual mother. She was born in 1933, two years after my actual mother. My mother was the daughter of an alcoholic garbage man, and was proud to have graduated from her technical high school. She took on a part-time job as a janitress to help pay for my college. Edelson's father was a dentist; at age thirteen she was taking Saturday classes at the Art Institute of Chicago, and her mother set up a home studio for her. She went to grad school in art, at New York University, in 1958, when few women did so. Our class divide throws a wrench in my spiritual mother fantasy. I'm reminded of the pang I felt when I read Alison Light's book on Virginia Woolf and her servants. In that divide, my family would have been on the side of the servants who cleaned Woolf's room of her own. But I still cannot totally discount Edelson's and my regional affinity. The intolerance for BS, the sick humor—I imagine she's impatient, like me, and loves stuffed cabbages.

Though well-known in feminist circles, Edelson was long marginalized by the international art establishment. Her celebration of the Goddess in much of her early work (in the 1990s replaced by cultural figures such as Lorena Bobbitt and Hollywood femme fatales, particularly Gena Rowlands in *Gloria* [1980]) has probably played a big part in that. In her 2012 article "Goddess: Feminist Art and Spirituality in the 1970s," art historian Jennie Klein chronicles how, despite a renewed interest in '70s feminist art, both in the '90s and more recently, the influence of feminist spirituality has been largely ignored. The Goddess, according to Klein, is the "unacknowledged white elephant in the room of the feminist body of art."

To familiarize myself with '70s feminist spirituality, I watched a thirty-two-minute YouTube video from 1980, "Feminist Visions of the Future," which is a montage of statements by major players of radical second-wave feminism. I learned from Starhawk that belief in the Goddess is not an escape from the world. It is focused on the earth, relations with human beings, animals, plants, ecology. The experiential is privileged over gospel. According to Starhawk, religion is a form of poetry, a metaphor for reality and knowing ourselves. Mary Beth Edelson urged me to embody and endow conventional symbols, such as the spiral, with a sense of newness. Mary Daly convinced me that when one moves beyond the linearity of patriarchal vision, many things that appear disparate are in fact profoundly connected. Narrator Lola Dalton seduced me with a vision of a future where sin and guilt and sexual taboo no longer enslave us; where war, destruction, and hatred have no place or monetary support; where our differences as well as our sameness are celebrated, for all life is interlinked. I learned from Baba Cooper that only in a culture of radical consent will there no longer be rape of women or of the earth. Second-wave feminists admitted that women's spiritual history was unrecoverable, so they tapped into their subconscious and made shit up. Theirs was a utopian project of reimagining the past to reinvent the future.

Edelson's goddess art awes me, particularly the series "Woman Rising," from 1973. Even though they begin with her naked body, these are not simply self-portraits. Edelson photographed herself with concentric circles painted on her midriff, as well as circles around her areolas, and then she altered the eight-by-ten-inch prints using oil paint, ink, watercolor, wax pencil, and collage, costuming herself as goddess or trickster. There is an urgent amateurism to the overpainting, evoking cheesy low-budget FX. The result is a mutable, fantastic body that references archetypal modes without being tied down to a predetermined system. "I also used my body as a 'found object' in these early works," Edelson writes, "with the intention of transforming the body into a 'found subject.'" She altered the same base photos over and over so that her reconfigured body becomes a material in the art process as much as it is content.

In one repeated pose, Edelson's hands boldly scoop up her breasts. This gesture is particularly comic in *Winter Sage: Viking with Time on Her Hands*. Of another work from the series, *Seeing Double*, Edelson writes, "I am taking command of the act of looking in this performance by directing my gaze at the viewer with three pairs of eyes. Created before discussions of the male gaze were formulated, nonetheless, this issue is addressed here without the advantage of feminist theory that was yet to come." The subject of *Seeing Double* looks more like a space alien that has come to observe Earth than a woman subverting the male gaze. A big appeal of these photos is their relentless otherness. The goddess may take the shape of a human, but she is not humanized. Edelson's own eyes are painted over with red sclera and black blobs of fully dilated pupils. The second pair of eyes, replacing Edelson's breasts, is really one eye with two black irises, with white dots for nipple-pupils, floating in red sclera. This is the most femmy set of eyes, with spiky lashes surrounding. Beneath them, the concentric circles on Edelson's midriff act as a generator, fueling the alien being's probe (in my fantasy, at least). The third set of eyes hovers above Edelson, satellites with lines connecting them to the breast eyes. With their red sclera, these eyes appear to look directly at the viewer. I imagine them relaying information back to the breast eyes. It reminds me of my hypervigilance when walking down the street, scanning for signs of creepiness that might coalesce into an assailant. The satellite eyes recur in *Burning Bright*, 1973, but this time Edelson's face is collaged over with the head and legs of a tiger. Behind the tiger's ears another mysterious wide-set pair of eyes emerges. Dozens of tiny warrior eyes swarm across Edelson's body. The image is cut off at the top of Edelson's thighs but the warrior eyes scurry into the bottom margin. They avoid the concentric circles on Edelson's midriff, the gut—not the brain—being the center of power and primal wisdom. In *Winter Sage: Viking with Time on Her Hands*, arrows or probes shoot out of the eyes of Edelson's Viking helmet head. Curlicues shoot out of her/its mouth, ears, and cunt. In *The Art of Mary Beth Edelson* (2002) this image is reproduced in a section titled "Exercising the Demons."

In *Fashion Plate c. 500 B.C. II*, Edelson again eradicates her face—this time with crosshatching—and paints a pair of huge eyes on her upper thighs, a sort of pubic surveillance patrol. This image is based on another pose Edelson repeatedly uses—again she's naked, again circles are painted around her areolas, and concentrically on her abdomen. Here her upper arms extend at her sides, forearms raised at right degrees, fingers spread—a gesture that is simultaneously worshipful, beckoning, and repellant. Energy radiates from her masterful palms, suggesting a being who could toss you across the room with a flick of the wrist. She stands upright with her legs spread wide. Edelson: "My early works, standing with legs wide apart, challenged the notion that no penis equates to a lack. I presented myself as a powerful, self-defining person in this body."

Edelson uses this wide-legged stance in a group of 1973 images she's classified as the "Monstre Sacré": "SHE has many faces depending on who is looking at her. SHE is variously: the hand in the trap—the putrefied body—holy terror—the unimpenetrable [sic] devouring female of blood lust. [. . .] SHE is the offspring of women who have been raped, and her rage is insatiable. SHE is unveiled, and up close there are no illusions in her X-ray eyes, she even knows herself." Her vision is as terrifying as her bloodlust; the two are intimately intertwined. The titles of images in this series fizz with power and rage: *Nobody Messes with Her*, *Patriarch Piss*, *Red Kali*. In *Nobody Messes with Her* and *Patriarch Piss*, Edelson's head has been madly scribbled over into configurations that suggest a cyclone or explosion. In the former, her arms are encased in arching red demon legs that sprout from her shoulders while in the latter, her arms are used to hang decapitated male heads dripping with blood. In *Red Kali*, SHE stands triumphant on the body of a quickly sketched man, his head and her left foot extending beyond the frame for her rage is too great to be boxed in by the photo's right-angled reality. *Red Kali* references both the fearsome Hindi goddess and female vengeance archetypes. In the late '60s Edelman participated in a five-year Jungian seminar. Though she eventually abandoned the Jungians, she was deeply impressed with the concepts of the collective unconscious and archetypes. Through ritualistically restaging mythological images from a range of cultures Edelson was, in her own words, "summoning Goddess to make house calls." Or as Lucy Lippard put it, "She re-mythologizes at the same time she de-mythologizes."

The Art of Mary Beth Edelson begins with a timeline of her life, paired with a timeline of what was happening in politics, popular culture, feminism, civil rights activism, and significant world events. This double time frame underscore's Edelson's commitment to collectivity and community, how she considered herself to be a product of a larger social network. The span of 1968–1974 was an enormously productive time for Edelson. In 1968 she moved to Washington, D.C., where she organized the first National Conference for Women in the Visual Arts (1972), and she "officially abandon[ed] painting for conceptual art making." By painting, she's referring to the abstract expressionist style she was taught in grad school at NYU. If she was influenced by mainstream conceptual art practices, the timeline doesn't note it. The timeline focuses, instead, on developments in feminist art. Besides the "Women Rising" series, Edelson created and published *Some Living American Women Artists/Last Supper* (1971), a collage poster commemorating under-recognized women artists, which she distributed to women's centers and conferences, and reproduced in feminist publications. That same year she orchestrated a collaborative experiment called *22 Others* (1971–1973) in which she invited Twenty-two friends and associates to her studio to discuss her work and to each suggest a piece they'd like to see her produce, and then she followed their instructions. In 1972 she launched *Story Gathering Box*, whose aim was to create a "collective mythology." Edelson invited audience members to write the answers to a series of questions such as "What did your mother teach you about women?" or "What was it like to be a boy?" The cards with their written answers were subsequently gathered by category in wooden boxes, and displayed on tables flanked by stools so visitors could peruse them. Edelson's projects from this era exemplify what Lucy Lippard characterized in 1980 as "the three major structures feminism has contributed to recent art": "ritual; collaborative/anonymous/collective methods of art-making and responding to audiences; and public media strategies designed to change the image of female experience." The radicalism of these collaborative works is sneaky. They are so process-oriented, so community-centered, so politically motivated that they move beyond the dualism of "good" or "bad" art, subverting my knee-jerk judgement mechanism, subverting the "white box" gallery machine they were designed in reaction to. In 1975 Edelson moved back to New York, she continued her commitment to collectivity, joining AIR Gallery, the first feminist cooperative art gallery. In 1977 she became a founding member of Heresies Collective, which published *Heresies: A Feminist Publication on Art and Politics*—a journal so influential and visible that even in Indiana I got my hands on it. Until recently, she was still visiting colleges and directing public rituals.

The unruliness of Edelson's Goddess images is thrilling. In the '80s I read every goddess book I could get my hands on. My studies profoundly changed my relationship to religion and other patriarchal systems such as Western philosophy. I learned how metaphors imprison us. Women = darkness, passivity, constriction. Men = light, action, expansion. I learned that language is a battlefield, and how I use words is never neutral. You either re-inscribe the status quo or blow it apart. Radical feminist linguists, such as Julia Penelope and Dale Spender, were a fierce bunch, determined to create a new system of logic that would reshape the world. The unrepentant eros of goddess culture influenced my first novel, *The Letters of Mina Harker*, in a big way.

The eponymous Mina is an immoral goddess figure who inhabits Dodie's body and lives beyond the rules of conventional society. She's a ravenous sexual being who, not being human, is so huge and excessive she can consume all of culture into her terrifying maw. As Edelson did in her goddess photos, I constructed Mina using collage and appropriation. Writing her was exhilarating. Dodie, on the other hand, is portrayed as a frightened little worm trying to conform to social expectations that Mina continuously fucks up. To my writing friends, I talked about my appropriation of vampire lore and sappy erotic thrillers and Freud's hysterics, but I never mentioned the debt I owe to goddess culture. To own up to the Goddess would have been an embarrassment. If only I were familiar with Edelson back then. Her confidence and entitlement would have served me well.

I approach Edelson's work with a mixture of excitement and mourning. All of her art, at its core, is a form of collage—the altered photos, sculptures, rituals, community-sourced work. She thrusts me back to the utopian spirit of second-wave feminism. Only through a revolution in consciousness could the patriarchy be overthrown—and these women believed that their glorious collectivity was going to make that happen. Of all the things global capitalism has stolen from us, perhaps the worst is a sense of hope. I mourn that hope, but also on a more pragmatic level, how can anybody consider first-generation feminist art and not mourn the recent passing of Carolee Schneemann and Barbara Hammer, both of whom were underappreciated by the mainstream art machine. The artist monographs I own on Edelson's work—*Seven Cycles: Public Rituals* (1980) and *The Art of Mary Beth Edelson*—are self-published, which is both awesome and sad.

From a videotaped conversation between Edelson and Schneemann, printed in *The Art of Mary Beth Edelson*:

Mary Beth: Well, we were pioneers, the way you approached the physicality of the female body from a woman's perspective in the United States in the '60s was ground breaking.

Carolee: Well, pioneers will be punished. None of that work is collected. None of it sold—none of it. The appreciation comes in the form of a mythology that grows up around your being useful to other artists.

In 2002, when this conversation was published, Edelson had a thriving career in Europe but no gallery in the US. Then in 2007 curator Connie Butler exhibited five of her collages in the germinal show "WACK!: Art and the Feminist Revolution," including her most famous piece, a reworking of Leonardo da Vinci's *Last Supper* titled *Some Living American Women Artists*, 1972, which features Georgia O'Keefe as Christ. Subsequently, New York's Museum of Modern Art purchased all five collages. Edelson, represented by David Lewis Gallery in New York, now has shows coming out of her ears. From her 2019 exhibition schedule: *Mary Beth Edelson: Shape Shifter*, David Lewis Gallery; *Laid Bare in the Landscape*, The Nevada Museum of Art; *Nobody Messes with Her*, Kunsthalle Münster; *Half the Picture: A Feminist Look at the Collection*, Brooklyn Museum; *Men of Steel, Women of Wonder*, Crystal Bridges Museum of American Art; *Art After Stonewall*, Grey Art Gallery and Leslie-Lohman Museum; *Feminist Avant-Garde of the 1970s: Works from the Verbund Collection* (touring exhibition). But at eighty-six, Edelson's health is not so great. When I recently commented to an artist friend Susan Bee that Edelson was having a moment, Susan told me that Edelson was in a nursing home in New Jersey, with dementia. In February Edelson was awarded the Women's Caucus for Art Lifetime Achievement Award, but she has no idea she got it. Susan shook her head and said that Edelson wasn't the only woman artist who was having a moment but who is unaware of her latest achievements. Not enough recognition and what comes is too late—this is the typical career path of radical feminist artists, especially those whose work focuses on sexuality and the body.

On YouTube I watch a two-part interview with Edelson from 2013. At eighty, she's still vivid, with an understated sensuality. She's trim with short spiky hair, dressed in a black T-shirt and wide-legged pants. Long cascades of feathers hang from her ears. She talks about how on the street she makes eye contact with those who tend not to be looked at, who are made to feel invisible. She gives a tour of her amazing SoHo loft, which has since been dismantled. The Feminist Institute Digital Exhibit Project photographed the entire studio with a 360-degree camera, and the resulting spherical images are available online at Google Arts & Culture. Edelson is not in any of the photos. It's just her living stuff and her "over 25,000 protest posters, wall drawings, correspondence, artworks and other ephemera." All this miraculous materiality abstracted to pure, woozy 3D images that I have much difficulty navigating.

To suggest spiritual transformation, in many photos Edelson dissolves her body, covering it with stippling or swirling spirals—and in the late 1970s black and white photographs of herself nude in natural landscapes, ghosting her form through long exposures and swaddling herself in transparent cloth. But in *Dematerializing*, 1975, she gouges the paper over and over with a sharp point. Though the image is occluded, the wounding of the paper heightens the photo's physicality. Thus, the violence of Edelson's process suggests a resistance to her own erasure. The Googlizing of Edelson's studio, while an amazing feat, evokes the tragedy of an irretrievable past. When I spy one of her naked goddess photos, I long to reach back to a kinder, kinkier, crazier, more naive time, when sex and spirituality and politics were linked, when women painted their bodies and ran around naked together. An entire generation of feminist visionaries will soon be gone. It's time for their successors to stop bashing that past and to begin to reimagine it.

Laugh and Cry

On Ugo Rondinone's Clowns

with Kevin Killian

Dodie Bellamy: One of the most obvious (and therefore most commonly noted) things about Ugo's work is how open to interpretation it is, how he's very precise in the construction of the work, but then he puts it out there and backs away. For me, this allows layers of psychological/emotional resonances to happen between the viewer and the work. When I look at his work, I feel like my unconscious is being played.

Looking at images of previous iterations of this exhibition in Rotterdam, Rome, and Shanghai, I'm taken by how site-specific they are, how some elements are repeated, some switched out. In Rotterdam the giant clown shoes hung on the walls of the same gallery the clowns were scattered about in. But here in Berkeley, the shoes are in a smaller separate room you pass through in order to reach the clowns. How does this separating of shoes from clowns impact you?

Kevin Killian: I wonder if it reflects a model of scarcity politics? Only four pairs of shoes, and then you go into the big room and see so many clowns without shoes. What does it signify? That there's not enough for everybody to go around. Or, symbolically, maybe it means that—not everybody is gonna become a star. They're performers, right? All of them want to become stars! Dozens of clowns, and only four pairs of shoes to share among them.

Four pairs! It's like Mount Rushmore—but for clowns. Only four presidents got to make it onto Mount Rushmore. And how many presidents have we had? 45, right? Some people call Trump "45" rather than speaking his name. How many clowns are there?

DB: Forty-five!

KK: Can it be a coincidence? No way!

DB: Of course I think of the meme that was going around Facebook recently that was titled "A Brief History of 45 Presidents of the United States," and which was illustrated by face emojis of 43 identical white men, followed by one black man, and ending with a clown face. The disparity between the number of shoes versus clowns never crossed my mind. The shoes are so powerfully metonymic that for me they simply represented the state of clownness, they're so colorful and bigger than life, yet rather sad and worn. And constructed with such care! There's tenderness in their hand-stitched patches. I was reminded of an older era when things were cherished and mended and repurposed.

Since this was the first room we entered, the hanging shoes had the feel of an antechamber to a ritual space, where you remove clothing/attitudes to enter sacred time. Though I wouldn't be so corny or overdetermined as to call the room of clowns "sacred." What feeling did you get entering the hall of clowns?

KK: Impressed how lifelike they seem, and how exquisitely drawn these clowns' faces are! They put me in mind of Watteau's "Pierrot" of 1719. Watteau's sad clown at least had the energy to stand up straight. These clowns are all "at rest," catching forty winks, reading books; staring into space, or propped up against walls, they're on a work break. Maybe clowns are like children, not yet caught up in the workforce and the labors of late capitalism. These clowns seem particularly removed from the hurly-burly of circus life. They receive some benefits, like their beautifully sewn costumes; they wear the abstracted look of aesthetes.

DB: Watteau's Pierrot seems painfully conscious of the viewer's gaze. He has a sort of deer in the headlights look to him, whereas Ugo's clowns seem totally self-absorbed in their interior lives, unaware they're being observed. So the viewer is in this perverse position of being an intrusive voyeur. As in the epistolary novel, where the reader is privy to letters that weren't meant for them, here the viewer is gawking at what feels extraordinarily private. Walking through the clowns, for me, was both intriguing and uncomfortable.

KK: In the last couple shows at BAMPFA, curators have prominently hung one of their treasures, Alexander Calder's gouache "Circus Scene" from 1926. In Calder's three ring circus, horses prance around one ring, elephants stand on hind legs and circle each other, and other spangly humans take center stage, while the clowns loom close to the audience as if to judge their reactions. They're ombudsmen, perhaps, representing ourselves to the performers and the performers to us. Something of that limbic state, of existing in two worlds at once, so not wholly of either, clings to Ugo's clowns as well. They're here, but in another sense, they're absolutely elsewhere—the waiting in the wings feeling so common to performers, where you're not really alive till you're out there under the lights.

Then there's the audience participation aspect. People seem to expect that at the Berkeley Art Museum—maybe at museums everywhere nowadays.

DB: The audience participation was one of the most startling aspects of the exhibit. One high school girl was sitting on the floor, leaning against the wall, right next to a clown, texting on her cellphone. Then she extended her legs and twisted her body to mimic the pose of the clown, and her friend took a photo. Everyone I talked to who visited the show witnessed something similar. Having the work at ground level seemed to give such permission, plus guards weren't overly protective, weren't rushing up to people telling them to keep their distance. But since the clowns felt so vulnerable, so unaware, so utterly unable to protect themselves, this colonizing behavior of the audience was also disturbing.

I find it fascinating the way you keep connecting Ugo's clowns back to the circus. Maybe it's because I've never been to a circus, but for me they resonated much more metaphorically as representing the masks/costumes of the persona, and even when these characters are limp in private repose, they can't discard those masks/costumes. Their faces are masks. There's a sense that neither can they ever find true solitude nor connection.

I'm reminded of the uncanniness of wax museums, and since these clowns were cast from real people, my mind starts tripping back to Hammer horror films, where in any wax museum there's inevitably a sentient being trapped inside one of those wax figures. In this case I felt like it was impossible for me not to project myself into the figures; I became the one trapped inside.

People were also interacting with the circular rainbows, getting their pictures taken in front of them. You even followed suit and had me photograph you in front of one!

KK: I love the feeling of power you get from imagining yourself as the center of a rainbow planet or something.

DB: They're wonderfully vibrant, but due to their concentric circles, they flicker back and forth between halo and target. It's exciting the way this work keeps calling up oftentimes conflicting emotional registers.

KK: Then walking into that room with five thousand drawings of rainbows and unicorns and whatnot . . . Inspirational sayings, cries from the heart, the hope that children feel despite world conditions. It was overwhelming. Staggering number of "feels," and even so, some individual images stand out—every time one visits, one sees particular examples of genius or kitsch one hadn't noticed before. "UGO" in colored letters—endearing familiarity of the first name address, as one who might address Picasso as "Pablo." The lavender cat with wings, bewildered by a flood of flying blue hearts hovering in the air above. The fatalistic simplicity of the words cresting one rainbow: "Breathe Walk Die." One pot of gold has the word "GOOD" painted across its bulge, heavy and black in a field of fleecy grass.

In that room one has the strange feeling that there are too many drawings to look at. The ones pinned to the wall twenty feet up are surely out of reach; frustrating perhaps, but maybe the lesson one learns is that one goes through life missing 97 percent of everything—and it's OK?

DB: When I heard about the rainbow drawings by children, I have to admit, I groaned, it sounded so saccharine. But I agree with you, the excess of it is wonderful, and on a sheer visceral level, the brightness made me giddy. The piece brings up issues around community and context, how one kid's drawing of a rainbow stuck on a refrigerator with magnets is cute and sentimental, and that's about it. But a whole room of them, floor to ceiling, is a marvel. It's like when we went to see the Monarch butterflies roost in Santa Cruz, adorning the eucalyptus trees with thousands of flickering wings.

I kept clinging to the optimism of these rainbows when we entered the final dark diary room, which is so baldly about loneliness, surveillance, despair, people sleeping with lights on that don't illuminate anything. The bold white letters on black background are hard to read, and there is so much language, so many panels, that standing there taking the piece in becomes an act of endurance. Like the shoe room, this too felt like an antechamber to a ritual space, like in the myth of Inanna, where the goddess is stripped of everything and descends to the underworld and is totally undone, in order to be reborn anew. So I kept flashing on the rest of the show as a sort of rebirth.

KK: Does the world just make you laugh?

DB: Well, laugh and cry.

7

Cinderella Syndrome

after Ellen Cantor

When I was a teen my mother called me Cinderella because of our battles over housework—scrubbing the bathtub, vacuuming, washing dishes. Though I did enjoy ironing during summer breaks. On a bright, lazy afternoon my mother would set the ironing board up in the living room. Due to my incompetence, she would give me only the simplest items, like pillowcases, and we would take turns sprawling on the couch and ironing as we watched the soaps together. For a couple of precious hours we liked one another. On school mornings, before dawn she'd barge into my room shouting, "Cinderella, get your ass out of bed!" "Come on, Cindy, get up!" Every pragmatist, including my mother, knows how to return the romance of Cinderella to its most banal component: her domestic labor. But I was a girl with her head in the clouds. I had no plans on how to escape the working class femininity I was born into. I just refused it.

College was a continuation of that refusal. I wanted to do drugs, have sex, read books, and be left the fuck alone. Cinderella never wanted to go to grad school. Grad students were dowdy, pinched and sexless as they clenched their stacks of books/briefcases in the Indiana University library elevator—or hunched over them in tiny carrels that were tucked away on the upper floors along with the perverts who stalked and flashed coeds. After I got my BA, I stayed in Bloomington because I had no idea what else to do, and compared to the Rust Belt where I was raised, it was paradise. Jobs were hard to come by. Wives of doctoral students got all the good ones, landing secretarial positions that required masters degrees and knowledge of a foreign language. At first I sweated in a hairnet and hideous yellow uniform in a dorm cafeteria. Then I moved to the lesser hell of the file room of the library, a job so tedious it was the only one in the library that didn't require work-study. See Cinderella in a windowless basement, perched on a stool hunched over acres of long skinny boxes containing book check-out slips, arranging them by call number—BF173.F74 O75; PQ2063.S3 A285; PR4746.E43 1931; PS1988.N29 1986; RC558.E43 1975—for agonizing minutes that slowly dripped into hours—BF698.9.C8 S57; PT2461.S3 A26—that dripped into despair. I wrote a poem in which I arose a triumphant goddess who climbed up amongst the boxes, spread my magnificent thighs, and pissed all over the cards. After I got grad school financial aid I moved upstairs to the circulation desk where I shot the shit with the cool kids, and the hours danced away.

I was determined I was never going to be tamed. When I was in my mid-twenties I made friends with a woman my mother's age. She was having an affair with a college professor, and she told me about the great old people sex she was having. When I reciprocated with the great young people sex I was having, she said she was amazed all those men would have sex with me, given how big I was. I was definitely a squirrel fur slipper kind of gal—though I own a glass slipper I bought on eBay in memory of the glass slipper I had as a child; it was as part of the packaging for my Cinderella watch. I quickly grew bored with the watch, but the slipper I fondled and fondled. It totally filled my seven-year-old palm and you could look through its thick transparency to a blurred world. I had big flat feet that cracked when I walked barefoot. I imagined them shrinking and arching into perfect daintiness, twirling across a gleaming parquet ballroom floor in total command of their fragile, precarious, blister-producing encasements. I also own a vintage Disney Cinderella figurine I got at a yard sale, back in the early '80s when I was married to my first husband. The tip of her ceramic nose has chipped off; otherwise she is a slick shaft of turquoise cream and gold. If I lay her on her side, she is the same length as her slipper, a vertiginous disruption of scale. According to megocollector.com, the watch was made by Timex and the slipper was plastic. It is hard to accept that my memory could be so wrong—but at seven I lived in magic, and magic knows not the difference between plastic and glass.

One morning, around the time I acquired the glass slipper my mother was in the basement, doing laundry—I was above her on the stairs and I asked her for something and she said no—or she told me to do something I didn't want to do—whatever she was saying I didn't like, didn't like it at all, and I called her a wicked old stepmother. "You keep talking that way, Missie, and I'm gonna wash your mouth out with soap," she yelled. And then she banned me from watching *The Little Rascals*, my favorite show, for it was the mean stepmother in the series that appealed to my fantasies of abuse. I probably got a few stern slaps across the ass as well.

Cinderella's beloved mother is dead, but the mother's spirit returns in the guise of a protectress: a fairy, a hawk who rewards Cinderella with a glowing star on her forehead, a gentle cow whose ears produce sustenance, a crab, an enchanted fish. The evil stepmother cooks and eats the fish, but Cinderella finds the bones and buries them, and over the grave a magical swing appears. She sits on the swing and sings to make it sway, and her song is heard by a passing prince. Cinderella plants a twig on her mother's grave, which grows into a hazel tree. When she cries about not going to the ball, the tree shakes down a golden dress and golden shoes for her to wear. This happens three times.

When I was a child, Cinderella was a redhead, like me, the blue of her gown so pale it looked translucent, the airy blue of fairy wings. Then Disney changed her to blonde, saturated the blue, and chiseled her some cheekbones. Unlike Cinderella, whenever I dress up, I feel like a dog in a tutu.

I fell in love with my first husband at a New Year's Eve party in Chicago. He was wearing suspenders and roller skates. Our first date lasted four days. His apartment in Pilsen was a dump, the gas heater spraying black soot across the wall. His sailor pants had a double row of buttons down the front, and when I gave him a blowjob, the coarse navy wool scratched my cheek. He was uncircumcised, which made him and his penis seem complicated. In a good way, I told myself. He didn't talk much, but there was this purity about him that was awesome—and he was always ready for sex or dancing—we went to a huge disco with whirling colored lights, and when people asked us our names, he said Ricky and I said Lucy. He was 29 years old and before me had only fucked once—and it's not like women weren't willing. His hair was dark and his lips were full and he was handsome as hell. I moved my luggage from my parents' house in Northern Indiana, and spent the rest of my month-long vacation with him. But then I realized I was five weeks pregnant—fallout from getting shitfaced drunk while playing pinball with an Australian tourist—and I had to go back to San Francisco to get Medi-Cal for the abortion. My future husband was wonderfully supportive, and though my excitement for him was already sagging, his attitude towards my shameful condition convinced me I'd found a gem, a prince who would recognize me for my true self.

Cinderella is one whose attributes are unrecognized, or one who unexpectedly achieves recognition or success after a period of obscurity and neglect. Her foot slides into a slipper made of glass, of gray squirrel fur, of gold, of golden fish scales; her foot slides into a sandal. Imposters cut off their toes, their heels. Doves point out the blood and peck out their eyes. Sometimes it's not a slipper at all but an anklet, a ring, or a bracelet that is the key to Cinderella's identity. A woman who lives among ashes is considered dirty and uncouth. Thus the prince, slipper in hand, must see her in that state, must accept her degradation. First there's the piston motion of foot after foot after foot into a fancy slipper, then the prince recognizes Cinderella's true self and slides his cock into Cinderella's fur slipper, and then.

By the end of February, I'd sold most of my stuff and moved back to Chicago to be with him. We were wed at sunrise on the grass, in Lincoln Park, overlooking Lake Michigan. It was a drizzly day and mosquitoes swarmed my arms and legs, and I said my vows through this god-awful itching. After we were married, my first husband told me that government agents were following him in semi-compact cars, and that he always flew under a fake name so they couldn't track his movements. Panic wrestled with denial, and my heart shouted STOP! THE SHOE IS TOO TIGHT.

We found an apartment in Logan Square, the bottom floor of a large two-flat. The building had been condemned, and the owners, who lived above us, bought it from the city for $1, with the agreement that they would fix it up. I was convinced the place was haunted by a woman with long brambly hair. I'd catch glimpses of her at the foot of our bed in the middle of the night, would see her shadow quivering under the bathroom door while I was in the bath. Since my first husband was a fireman, he'd be gone for stretches of time, sometimes for days. It was brutal when I was alone there, holding back terror while trying to write. For inspiration, I took notes on his firefighting manual, with all its great terms like jaws of life, a hydraulic contraption that gnaws open mangled vehicles in order to free those trapped inside. I wanted to put jaws of life into a poem, wanted to strip it of context, make it about me, life with its big jaws coming after me. As I said, my first husband loved sex. He always made me come before he did, yet the process was starting to bore the shit out of me. The jaws of life would save me both from matrimonial blahs and brambled haired women. This anxious dull pressure was building, and one night it got so bad I banged my head against the wall until it bruised. The jaws of life would lick the bruises from my forehead, free me. But it never made its way into a poem. Recently, encountering for the first time the panels of Ellen Cantor's *Cinderella Syndrome* in a darkened gallery in San Francisco, I saw to my surprise how something of the brutal poetry I experienced in marriage she was able to capture—the jaws of life making their way into a poem at last, and it was not mine.

My first husband was a proxy to wonder. His was a world in which donkeys shit gold. I never stopped loving his sweetness, his otherworldliness that drove employees and his family crazy. But sharing a checkbook with him was maddening. He refused to tell me when he wrote a check because that was "private," which resulted—duh—in overdrafts. Tired of my complaints, my friends said, "Get your own checking account." My first husband believed that clockwise was spiritual and counterclockwise was satanic, so when he wrote, he made sure he only formed his letters in a clockwise direction. He felt the same way about gold versus silver, and my love of silver jewelry troubled him greatly. He read that for optimal digestion, one should eat only fruit in the morning, so he'd sit up naked in our bed with half a watermelon in his lap, mucking up the sheets with seeds and sticky pink juice. Over and over I asked him not to do this, but he did it anyway, and I found myself yelling at him to stop making such a mess and to put on some fucking clothes, just like my mother would have.

When I couldn't take any more of my husband or the bramble-head ghost, I'd escape to my favorite coffee house, Caffe Pergolesi, and write poems in my journal. I wrote:

> wanting the walls to soften
> to sink in
> around my shoulders
> plaster down.

I wrote:

> my face turned to the wall,
> like a dead woman's mirror.

I wrote:

> This dream wouldn't rate
> any higher than half a star.

Caffe Pergolesi closed in the early '90s after the owner's son was murdered by Jeffrey Dahmer. Boiling water poured into a hole in his skull. Dahmer called Weinberger's death exceptional because he was the only victim to die with his eyes open.

After nine months, my first husband quit the fire department and we moved back to San Francisco into an apartment on Hermann, across the street from the Mint—the place where they manufacture the money. We slept on an air mattress, which my husband liked to belly-flop onto. When I'd whine don't, you're going to break it, he'd get back up, let out a big WHOOPIE! and flop even harder. Of course it eventually sprung a leak. Each night we'd blow it up but as we tossed and dreamt of a life where we had money for a real bed, it would slowly deflate to slushy gel. Eventually we just slept on the floor, him snoring away, me clenched with rage. I was a freelance graphic artist for slide production companies back then, which paid well, but the industry was collapsing and gigs were getting more and more erratic. My first husband took a job in the headquarters of a spiritual group he was involved in, and only made $500 a month, not nearly enough to live on, even in the early '80s. I was partially funding him—something I hadn't agreed to. More rage. Eventually he switched to cab driving, which brought in more money, but his maniac driving resulted in all these moving violations. Somehow he avoided losing his license by constantly going to traffic school.

Unconstrained by any sort of anatomical accuracy Cinderella swims through stars. A wash of pastels undulates across a matte field, across afternoons filled with hot pink pussy evening twilight and blue clear skies, all yellow longing vanquished. Once—twice—thrice—animal spirits leap about on the sidelines, calling her out, cheering her on. They recognize the unrecognizable in her. "Beware what you wish for," they shout. "Beware what you promise. Beware what you utter."

My first husband was an elemental being, terse to the point of blankness, brimful of inconsistencies, and plotted with a baffling lack of logic. He believed he possessed the power of invisibility, that he could cloak himself and disappear. And he did disappear on me. Often. Whenever I looked behind me I expected to find him gone. Like the time we went to a Linda Ronstadt concert. It was in an outdoor auditorium and I had the tickets. As we neared the ticket booth I turned around and no husband. I frantically looked for him everywhere, pushing my way through the oncoming crowd. Finally when it was time for the concert to begin, I gave up and went to our seats, where I found him lounging on the bleachers. I started screeching—by this time in our marriage I was screeching a lot—where were you I looked everywhere for you how did you get in without a ticket. He was this big goose sitting there, smiling blankly, my anger like beads of water bouncing off his waxy head.

Once when we got in a monstrous fight—WHY HOW WHERE-FOR WHEN—and I attacked him with a mayonnaise jar—I HATE YOU YOU ARE RUINING MY LIFE—my first husband told me that he couldn't love me the way I wanted him to. "Get out," I screamed, and then I picked up on my halted on-and-off affair with M., another writer in the scene. I invited M. into my bedroom, though I'm not sure what state of inflation the mattress was in—and we had a fuckfest. Eventually my first husband begged me to take him back, and admitted that he'd been sleeping in the basement beneath our apartment. He asked me if I'd been faithful—he was obsessed with monogamy—while he was gone and I said—"Of course I have"—even though I suspected he'd heard M. and I pounding through the floorboards. "Are you sure?" he said. "Yes," I murmured. I called up M. and put him on hold again. For now.

My first husband would sit in Golden Gate Park absolutely still and squirrels would climb along his arms and shoulders, and so our apartment became infested with squirrel fleas that rode home on my husband's clothing. There were warning in the paper about squirrels harboring fleas that carried plague. I scratched the inflamed bites on my legs, so pissed I felt light headed. Being married to a magical being was untenable, yet I stayed and stayed because I was afraid of being alone. Yet being with him was being alone.

Cinderella's experience of life is atemporal, her memories a series of overlapping, even contradictory tableaux. *Think about your husband have bad dreams be haunted.* After we got divorced I enjoyed hanging out with my first husband, he was so calming. I remember us sitting on the grass in some park, not talking much, just taking in the sunshine like a couple of lizards and my chronic anxiety melting away. My mother said my marriage was a failure, that I had failed. It took her years to accept my second husband; it's like she didn't want to invest in another fucked up whim of mine. Eventually Kevin won her over and she declared him the best son-in-law in the world. My mother liked me better as the middle class person Kevin shaped me into than the working class girl she raised.

Cinderella runs from the ball with life's jaws nipping at her heels. She talks to animals and pumpkins; she doesn't eat them. During sex or dreams she fractures into a series of elongated ellipses, football-shaped diamonds cut and polished to mimic the Marquise of Pompadour's perfect lips. Lazy and labial, that is she. She never revises; she collages over, sloppily burying the shameful the unwanted. The past's edges show through reminding us that nothing is ever ever final. Other framings still exist—layers of racing voices and images—she uses quick strokes to capture them—the personal—NEED—the cultural—SLUT—the marital—WHAT THE FUCK. Cinderella is always naked, and instead of putting her stuff away she piles one thing on top of the other. Aprons float through indefinite space. She is inconsistent in her extremes—either mumbling or shouting, either too personal or absent, smudged with soot, imagining her broom as a gun. She paints with soot, paints herself into a corner with soot. Consciousness flickers as if gravity has unhinged itself and she bounces and bounces until nothing's there.

Unbearable Intimacies

On Reading Marie Darrieussecq's *Being Here Is Everything: The Life of Paula Modersohn-Becker*

One summer in Los Angeles, Hedi El Kholti—my and Marie Darrieussecq's editor at Semiotext(e)—gave me this book. "Here," he said as he handed it to me. "I love this book." When I returned to San Francisco I threw it in a pile and forgot about it. But then it somehow moved to the bathroom and I was hooked. Like in many Victorians in San Francisco, my bathtub and toilet are in two separate rooms. The toilet room, no bigger than a closet, along with my office, is on an enclosed back porch. As I sit at my desk, the bathroom is behind me. If someone's visiting and wants to use the facilities, I need to get up and go to another room, to give them some privacy. There's a litter box wedged in next to the toilet, and sometimes one of the cats will sit in the box beside me, doing their business, and I feel like such an animal. They don't understand most of what I do, but this they get. Marie Darrieussecq: "We work and we are bodies" (147). Throughout all my writing the shadow of dejecta looms.

Being Here Is Everything is very much about the body, the aliveness of Paula Modersohn-Becker at the turn of the 20th century, and the bodies of the women she painted, especially the nudes, finally freed from the imposed metaphors of "centuries of the male gaze" (79). Modersohn-Becker's nursing babies look like real babies, and they're held the way real women hold nursing babies. Since Modersohn-Becker died of complications from pregnancy, all these images of mother-child fusion are infused with tragedy. Darrieussecq enters an almost unbearable intimacy with her subject, mourning Modersohn-Becker's untimely death at the age of 31, longing to reach back through time and touch her which, of course, is impossible. I have no barriers to such intimacy as I hold her book with my panties around my ankles. It is a book that can handle my exposed ass. Through it I enter into what Julia Kristeva has termed a "jubilatory anality." When I was a girl I asked—why doesn't anybody go to the bathroom in the movies? The answer was—it's because you were born in the 1950s—just wait—the sitting on the toilet shot will become a cliché—the woman with her long twiggy legs pressed together, tiny ass ballooning against the porcelain seat—the question you should be asking is why don't women in the movies spread their legs when peeing or taking a shit, splayed crotch wafting disregard and funk.

At a small dinner party, I mention my angle would be that I read the entire book in the bathroom. Laughter ricochets throughout the room of artists and theorists. "Do you think that's bad taste?" I ask. Pam says, "Yes, and that's precisely why you should write it." Bathroom stories ensue. Geoff has a friend who got a job in tech, and his friend was grossed out when he saw a coworker taking his laptop into the toilet stall—but then he realized it wasn't just the one guy, they all did it. They also texted while standing at the urinal. I counter with how at San Francisco State women are always talking on the phones while on the toilet, but the worst was the student who would sit in the stall next to mine and shout at me questions about class. Anne scrunches up her face and says she can't imagine talking to a student in the bathroom.

While I've read magazines and bits of books in the bathroom, this is the first book I read there in its entirety. I read it slowly, over many months. I looked forward to it punctuating my daily. *Being Here Is Everything* is written in a series of vignettes, which allows Darrieussecq to quickly shift perspective from close up to expansive, to move freely between narrative, analysis, and exposition. Within the vignette's logic of accrual, time is fluid and circular, the past and present skittishly tapping against one another as in a recent Reddit joke of the day: *The Past, Present and Future walk into a bar. Things get tense*. In *Being Here is Everything* we get the history of portraiture, of female self-portraiture, the treatment of women artists then and now, the history of French art, of German art, the history of Germany. We get Modersohn-Becker's innovations in style and subject matter, how she painted the first ever female nude self-portrait: "The nude self-portrait of a woman, one on one with herself and the history of art" (126). No one produces in a vacuum, and Modersohn-Becker is presented as a figure in the crossroads of many layers of history. Each gesture she makes reverberates with larger forces. Beneath a vast German sky at the birth of the 20th century, the laughter of a young woman explodes into an array of vectors. Modersohn-Becker is both never alone and always alone, a product of her times who sees beyond her times, altering the history of women and art. We get an overview of the final seven years of her life, her complicated friendships with Clara Westhoff and Rainer Maria Rilke, her courtship and difficult marriage to painter Otto Modersohn, the time she spent in Paris and its influence on her painting (funded at first by an endowment from her uncle, then by Otto's robust art career), her frenzied productivity near the end (eighty paintings in 1906 alone). We get that in her lifetime, Modersohn-Becker only sold three paintings. The first sale was to Rilke, the second to artists Martha and Heinrich Vogeler, and the third to another friend, Frau Brockhaus—all of them used to subsidize Paula's 1906 relocation to Paris when she flees the claustrophobia of domesticity. After seven months she and Otto get back together, Paula gives birth to a girl and eighteen days later dies of a pulmonary embolism, a common pregnancy complication back then.

The vignette is the perfect form for bathroom reading—and for our digitally-fractured, ADHD-raddled now. A book consumed in discreet paragraphs which are placed next to one another, bits which pile up almost imperceptibly to reveal a larger whole. The vignette disrupts the notion of life as a narrative arc. Death and life are held simultaneously. With her novelist's eye for dramatic tension, Darrieussecq introduces Paula's death on the second page. "Let us not forget the horror that accompanies the wonder" (12). Her death beats through the text like a drum, creating a visceral sense of mortality, and rendering Modersohn-Becker's aliveness so bright I found myself rushing the book to my desk five feet away to scribble in the margins. Darrieussecq: "And then a self-portrait with irises. It is a tipping point, a perfect moment. Pure simplicity: this is me, these are irises. See: this is what I am, in colors and in two dimensions, mysterious and composed" (100). As I underline this passage, I wonder, *Is this what Hedi loves?*

Throughout, Darrieussecq asserts that Modersohn-Becker painted what she saw—local women, children, intimates, nature, herself. Regarding Modersohn-Becker's pregnant nude self-portrait—the first pregnant nude self-portrait in art history: "She paints what she sees in front of her: that being-there, that presence in the world, which happens to be pregnant" (138). I think of the meaty tranquility of all those nursing mothers the Modersohn-Becker painted, and it's obvious to me that had she lived, Modersohn-Becker would have painted the first nursing self-portrait, and this feels like a great loss to the history of art in the

Western world. Sitting on my porcelain throne I wonder—somebody must have painted the first nursing self-portrait, but who? To reiterate the purity of Modersohn-Becker's vision, Darrieussecq quotes from Rilke's "Requiem for a Friend," which he wrote a year after her death: "And at last you saw yourself as a fruit, you stepped out of your clothes and brought your naked body before the mirror, and you let yourself inside, down to your gaze, which remained strong, and didn't say: This is me, instead: This is" (127). In one particularly touching passage, Darrieussecq visits the Northern German countryside where Modersohn-Becker lived, and tries to see the landscape through the artist's eyes. "The birch trees, their black-and-white trunks tilting against the bright blue canal, the sky plunging into the water like a knife" (56). The landscape seems unchanged until Darrieussecq reminds herself that separating her viewing and Modersohn-Becker's are two world wars and the Final Solution. "Paula was born and died in an innocent Germany" (57). Darrieussecq concludes, "The forests are not the same as they were" (56). Elsewhere Darrieussecq writes: "Paula is a bubble between two centuries. She paints quickly, in a flash" (28). The Nazis seized seventy of her paintings from museums, some of which they hung in the 1937 *Degenerate Art* exhibition in Munich. Many did not survive.

Darrieussecq deftly includes herself in Modersohn-Becker's narrative—how she came to learn of the artist, her encounters with the paintings in person, how Modersohn-Becker's portrayal of a woman nursing is true to her own experience of nursing a child. But she never competes with Modersohn-Becker or overwhelms her, never tries to make the book her story. At the same time, she makes it clear that this is not an official version of Modersohn-Becker's life and art, but one woman's resonance with it. "And, through all these gaps, I in turn am writing this story, which is not Paula M. Becker's life as she lived it, but my sense of it a century later. A trace" (53). As I reach back and flush I appreciate Darrieussecq's integrity.

Writing about the self is not necessarily narcissistic—though, particularly with the rise of online "journalism," I could point to dozens of examples that are eye-rollingly so, where the grandeur of the self threatens to eclipse whatever it encounters. When one observes the self, if one stays true to what one sees there, the self becomes a portal for the rest of the world to rush into, a wavering point from which history past and present streams. Observing the self, one taps into the larger culture in which it is embedded. When Tongo Eisen-Martin visited my Writers on Writing class at San Francisco State, he spoke repeatedly about staying true to the moment in both writing and reciting poetry. He advised my students to follow the energy and to keep the ego out of it. He said that when you say to yourself, "This is working really well, I'm onto something here," it takes you outside the process, and your work fails. This rigor towards a vision that empties oneself is essential in self-portraiture. This emptying is the key to Modersohn-Becker's genius.

When I pick up *Being Here Is Everything* in all my humiliating materiality, I am *there*. Again and again the book returns me to my body. Sometimes there's cramping, sometimes the sweetness of ease. As I write at my desk, behind me is litter and soggy tissue from deluxe rolls purchased at Trader Joe's, urine flushed or not, the sudden stench of cat poo. Septic is Cockney slang for an American. I wonder if working on their laptops on the toilet brings the techies into their bodies—or if they're so far gone in abstraction they could be anywhere. I hope one of them watches porn, soundtrack piped in through Bluetooth earbuds, fist pumping cock in slippery slaps—grunt grunt—*here*.

Pushing and Pulling, Pulling and Pushing

with Kevin Killian

Dodie Bellamy: When I think of Mike Kelley, the first words that come to mind are: libidinal, fucked up, memory, and a sense of magic. There's the political as well, but I feel that's more of a ghostly presence behind other ghostliness that become embodied in his work. What are the first things you think of?

Kevin Killian: I love this idea about starting off with first things. Over and over again, we experience Kelley's work as a pained encounter with childhood memories. I wonder if it wasn't the shared experience of you, me, and Mike Kelley coming from Eastern- Midwestern and Eastern-Eastern childhoods and then forged by the shock of coming to California in particular that created for you and me, way back during the time of Kelley's inclusion in Paul Schimmel's germinal 1992 "Helter Skelter" exhibition at LACMA—that moment of utter recognition. What was the name of that show that we saw at Rosamund Felsen around that time, with all the stuffed animals?

DB: After a vigorous round of googling, I can say with certainty that was in 1990, his *Empathy Displacement* series. There it is, right in the name, displacement! I wrote about the show in my first book *The Letters of Mina Harker*.

Mike Kelley's opening at Rosamund Felsen Gallery—forty years ago Marilyn's famous calendar nudes were shot in this same studio, now it's hung with portraits of rag dolls a wall of them, human-sized black and white they loom above the actual dolls which lie on the floor in miniature coffins *representation has killed them* in one corner white-haired and tall as a legend John Baldessari stands in a bright blue shirt chatting with a couple of academic types … in another Mike Kelley's long graying hair is pulled back in a ponytail, his arm is being pumped by a corpulent man in a plaid leisure suit. There is a tiny door on each coffin over the face *an abyss that divides the axis of vision from the axis of things* a woman in camouflage stretch pants lifts one of the doors and peers in at the stuffed cotton expression then up at the canvas *without imaginative interiority a face is a nothingness* a guard rushes up and grabs her by the shoulder DON'T TOUCH THE COFFINS.

I wish I didn't feel like such a nerd back then and got somebody to introduce me to Kelley. I had to wait until 2008 to have my one and only conversation with him. But his work has been seminal to me ever since I first saw a drawing of his in Dennis Cooper's living room in Los Angeles. The stories we heard about him were legendary, going after the new lover of his former girlfriend with a gun . . .

KK: The stories scared me. The whole CalArts "Helter Skelter" thing scared me. They were all madmen. Felsen's was a gallery beautifully designed to show off Mike's work. You paraded from right to left, across an architectural space much much wider than it was deep. It looked like a stage space, meant for theater. Kelley was then into Grand Guignol horror elements, which were originally stage effects of the very early 20th century.

DB: Which makes me think about how the spaces in which they're shown affects these works. When we saw Kelley's retrospective at the Geffen, though it was marvelous and airy, and stunning to see his range and the resonances between his very different projects—it also was disconcerting to see such intimate work museumized. People I spoke with who saw the show at PS1, with its smaller, discrete rooms, said it seemed like a totally different show. In particular, for this Capp Street show, I'm wondering about the impact of displaying the yearbook reconstructions in such an intimate living space. On the walls they remind me of your parents' house on Long Island, framed images of you and your siblings, floor to ceiling, at all stages of your life. Capp Street's placement of yearbook reenactment scenes above the bed makes them seem both family photos and dream items—the domestic in tension with the fantastic, a quiet nightmare of dark rituals. Eerie!

KK: The Geffen, with its multi-level design, constantly had you going up ramps and stairs, and descending, but when you see similar work confined to the Ireland house, to the actual linearity of two floors, you are forced to deal, again, with the specter of childhood and the horror of being confined. But these feelings always arise when I'm at the David Ireland House.

DB: It's kind of like art immersion therapy! One more memory about the Geffen show. Since it was planned before Kelley's suicide, but opened afterwards, artist friends in LA said the opening felt more like a funeral than a party. Everyone was in shock, and therefore the sense of loss everywhere palpable in Kelley's work was intense, and forever changed my relationship to the work. It was hard to walk through it and not cry.

KK: What confuses me is the period in, say 2003, when we should have met Mike Kelley here in San Francisco at the Wattis.

Matthew Higgs remembers us well interacting with Mike. But since we have no memory of this, it's like it happened in another dimension, in one of Kelley's Kandor bell jars. I'm tying this in with a contemporary art project in which we all figured—Anne Collier's aura portraits, which do have that Kandor look. In a psychic shop in Oakland near Jack London Square, we were positioned in a chair and each photographed with grand colorful hazes streaming from our bodies. I remember mine was so dark, I had mine done again. Yours was swirls of blues and purples, but Mike's was oddly monochrome, a blue mist with a blob of purple near his right shoulder.

DB: The moment in *Pushing and Pulling, Pulling and Pushing* I keep going back to is the distressed plastic chick in the *Mechanical Toy Guts* installation, with a rod instead of wings through its shoulders, its blank white eyes, and those bits of feathers glued, out of place, to its feet. There's something about the discomfiture of textures that profoundly moves me in ways I cannot understand and have no control over. The overall feeling I had at Kelley's Geffen retrospective comes flooding back, where it was like Kelley was a virtuoso playing my subconscious, as if it were a violin. Kelley's ability to make texture miserable is so Joseph Beuys.

But you never did tell me, Kevin, what are the first things you think of when you hear Mike Kelley's name?

KK: I keep going back to Ed Smith's 1987 interview with Kelley in *Shiny International*. Childhood as Kelley tells Smith, is "the most interesting time period of sex because you're totally mystified. You don't know the full difference between the sexes so your idea of sex is really outlandish and fanciful. You spend all your time just trying to figure things out, what things did and as you get older it just becomes thinking about not what things do but what roles are. It gets narrower and narrower and narrower. When you're a kid it's actually about physicality and body and stuff, and you're really hooked into that because you have a body and you think about it. Horror films are always so sexual, they're all about body mutations. Everything's turning into fantastic sex organs." So that's what I think of first and last. Fantastic sex organs. Like the mechanical chick that you noticed—it's childlike and obscene at the same time.

10

The Kingdom of Isolation

In Disney's animated musical, *Frozen* (2013), Princess Elsa grows up hiding in shame because she's been told she's dangerous, not right. When she ascends to queen, a horrified populace discovers her wrongness, and she flees to a frozen wasteland. As she tromps through the snow, she sings "Let It Go," and her rage bursts free, building a glittering palace of ice, a frozen sublime. In Anne Walsh's video *Anthem* (2015–17), a roomful of postmenopausal women (plus a couple of elderly men) perform "Let It Go" in a series of discontinuous cuts. Each woman sings a line or two, and then another continues. There are choral sections and simple choreography. The women's haircuts, outfits, and locations change, but the song moves forward, without stopping, to its very end. A woman who seems to be their teacher plays the piano and directs them. The viewer is left to ponder: What is *Anthem* an anthem to? Aging? Mortality? The enduring repeatability of Disney schlock?

Composed of two parts, the music video plus a four-channel "anatomization" that provides close-ups of rehearsal dynamics and participants' bodies harvested from the twelve-week musical theater class Walsh enrolled in, *Anthem* is part of her ongoing exploration of the surrealist painter Leonora Carrington's 1976 novel *The Hearing Trumpet*. (Late in life Carrington met Walsh in Mexico City.) Set in a mystical old people's home, *The Hearing Trumpet* tracks the adventures of the elderly occupants through an apocalyptic upheaval that leaves their world turned on its axis; the equator is flipped to the North Pole, and what was once a lush paradise winds up located where Lapland formerly was. Like the characters in *Frozen*, the crones come to live in a land of ice and snow.

I first saw *Anthem* at Walsh's solo show at the Luggage Store in San Francisco in 2017. The video was rear-projected onto a glass wall. Its surface was so shiny that you could see yourself and the rest of the room reflected in it, so there was a merging of the then of the video and the now of the exhibition. My body and Anne's body, overlaid with the bodies of the women on the screen, glimmered with them. We were both meaty and immaterial. Arms lift in victory and greeting. *Let the storm rage on.* The video looped as Anne and I sat in weird collaged rolling chairs in the middle of the gallery, discussing our fears of aging. Susan Sontag: *Aging is a movable doom. It is a crisis that never exhausts itself, because the anxiety is never really used up. Being a crisis of the imagination rather than of "real life," it has the habit of repeating itself again and again. The territory of aging (as opposed to actual old age) has no fixed boundaries.*

It would be easy to film the seniors in the video as other, but Anne has inserted herself in the middle of them. She is the first to sing: "The snow glows white on the mountain tonight, not a footprint to be seen." She looks up to the ceiling, as if very disturbed. Behind her the backup singers come together in a tight circle, right arms above their heads, reaching toward the center, building the palace of ice. Anne, who teaches art at the University of California, Berkeley, becomes a middle-class East Bay woman of a certain age who takes random classes. She's younger than the rest of the crones and she's aging well, but

Anne's fate is their fate—their clunky choreography, questionable pitches, their stilted group bonding behavior, hers. Like them, she is exposed in her amateurism, alone in a group that never quite coalesces. Her flesh is falling, like everybody else's. *I'm never going back, the past is in the past.* These women have so much past, the floor buckles with the weight of it.

A kingdom of isolation and it looks like I'm the queen. A thick woman in jeans and long-sleeved knit top sings *I'm the queen* in an exaggerated sexy manner, with hand on cocked hip, as if she were Mae West or a drag queen. In the Kingdom of Isolation the swirling storm inside breaks through the queen's fleshy barrier and remakes the world. *My power flurries through the air into the ground.* The crones swirl their hands and make whooshing sounds because, being old and female, they are one with nature. Only in Ice-olation can a queen's passion roar; only there can she become the artist she was always meant to be, a great sculptress of frozen water. Who needs humans with their hearts all hot and pierceable. She is alone, pure, uncaring, a shivery genius. *The Hearing Trumpet* explores the shadow side of such pristineness— the earth is frozen, according to the priestess figure Christabel, because humans have renounced the Great Mother's pneuma (vital spirit, soul, creative force). "Her flight after the atomic war was the final nail in the coffin of this generation. If the planet is to survive with organic life she must be induced to return, so that good will and love can once more prevail in the world." The crones summon Hekate from the underworld for counsel. Choreographed arms fly up to the left, right, front. Hekate manifests in the form of a giant bumble bee. But how much power does a queen have if shunned by society? According to the poet and cultural critic Lisa Robertson, potentially a lot. In *Proverbs of a She-Dandy*, Robertson links menopausal women to 19th-century dandies. In 1821, the year Charles Baudelaire was born, so were the terms menopause and dandy. Robertson: "The distinctive stance of the Baudelairean dandy is the subtraction of all utility and all ambition from everyday life." She notes that the menopausal woman, no longer a part of a reproductive economy, is also beyond use value—and also freed of the constraints placed on women of childbearing age. The second section of Robertson's book is a series of proverbs. Proverb: SHE IS THE MASTERPIECE OF THE ANCIENT SUPERIORITY OF THE IMPRODUCTIVE. SHE NEITHER BEGETS NOR WORKS, BUT DRIFTS. She has entered what Robertson calls "the menopausal sublime," a radicality that threatens the social order. Proverb: AS SHE DRIFTS, SHE HUMS A LITTLE TUNE. WHAT IS THAT TUNE.

I know what it is: *Let it go, let it go, that perfect girl is gone . . .* In *The Hearing Trumpet* they're power-humming as well: *The Goddess hummed with a million voices and drops of honey fell like manna from the roof of the cavern. We were covered with a most delicious perfumed stickiness and were obliged to lick ourselves clean.*

The queen travels alone to a place where all is lost, and then her self is reborn. This is the way it's supposed to work. Monica Lewinsky in *Vanity Fair*: *As Haruki Murakami has written, "When you come out of the storm you won't be the same person who walked in. That's what this storm's all about."* "Let It Go" is an anthem for the woman beyond use value. Is she engaged in a mythic journey or merely making the best of a bad situation? Doris Lessing: *And we, the old ones, want to whisper into those innocent ears. "Have you still got your space? Your soul, your own and necessary place where your own voices may speak to you, you alone, where you may dream. Oh, hold onto it, don't let it go."*

According to pop psychology, a woman who ages well becomes more resilient. She possesses remarkable vigor, maintaining a modest sense of well-being until the final months before she dies. She is open, curious, and kind with herself. She says no to people and ideas that hold her back. She is quirky, imperfect, and unapologetic. She releases grudges and anxieties, picks herself up after setbacks, says a resounding yes to the world. When she needs it, she asks for help. She finds joy in the ordinary, experiencing the extraordinary right here and now in her body. Nothing about her is matronly or sexless. She exudes self-confidence and elegance. She knows how to dress for who she is. She eschews leggings, which are one of the most unflattering things a woman of her age could wear. She's in great shape, with healthy skin and a stylish haircut. She is feisty and not afraid of being alone. Her memory loss is offset by insight. She laughs a lot and shares her life lessons with younger people. She's a good listener. She keeps learning and improving. She takes classes, such as singing or something from the Fromm Institute for Lifelong Learning—a place where retired adults over fifty study with emeritus professors, the desire to learn the sole criterion for enrollment. My chiropractor, burned out on OkCupid, has enrolled in Ancient Mesopotamia in hopes of meeting a well-off widower. She's an expert on the human body, so she watches how men get up from their desk chairs. She's kept herself in good shape, and she doesn't want a debilitated partner. To age well, one volunteers. Working in her local animal shelter's thrift store saved my grieving mother. It gave her something to do and pulled her out of her deadly isolation. She made friends there, good friends who would drive her to chemo. A male volunteer became interested in her, and when I urged her to go for it, she screwed up her face and said, "I've had enough of them mens."

Men sometimes sing "Let It Go." It doesn't belong to them. Even though *Frozen* is marketed for children, when children sing "Let It Go," they seem ridiculously lacking in experience and understanding. "Let It Go" is not the song of a princess. It is the song of a queen. In fairy tales, queens are evil or absent. "Let It Go" represents the queen in her absence, the mature woman as an oppressive force, exiled to the Kingdom of Ice-olation. What appear as snowflakes to the naked eye are really little bees who do her bidding. (Bees often symbolize the divine feminine because they are ruled by queens.) Should the queen capture you, you are doomed unless you learn the secret to freedom, and that secret is you must spell out eternity with pieces of ice, which is ironic since the queen's land of ice and snow has been diminishing for centuries. *The Hearing Trumpet: The earth seemed to be limping around its orbit seeking balance in the new order.* As the queen's soil thaws, it releases methane, which contributes to an increased rate of global warming as part of a feedback loop. Soon there will be no place for frozen queens to go. The roots of the queen's trees are shallow, and as the ground thaws, the trees lose their footing and tilt helter-skelter, and thus her beloved black spruce and larch become a "drunken forest." Drunken trees may eventually die from their displacement.

After the chiropractor, after Sephora buying lipstick, in Illy drinking cappuccino. Sitting in front of the makeup mirror in Sephora confronting the aging fleshiness of my body, huge and untoned—ugh! Orangey-pink lip stains on white porcelain cup. An old woman walks in, her arms hung with Target bags—several of them—stuffed until bulging. She holds out a foot-tall clear plastic glass and says, "Water." The counter guy gives her a patronizing smile, then fills her glass from the faucet. She sips as she ambles out. She's too put together to be homeless—but she's out of it—yet charismatic enough to assemble a support staff like this barista who was so snotty to me just a few minutes ago. Proverb: THAT SHE EXISTS AND MOVES IN THE CITY IS AN AFFRONT TO THE WILL OF CAPITAL. COUNTLESS CLINICS ARE DEDICATED TO

PREVENTING HER APPEARANCE. I imagine her living in a garbage house, all the oxygen displaced by decades of accrual. Our own overflowing apartment. Why do I have so much more stuff—exponentially so—than when I was young. These shelves, these boxes crammed with god knows what, are the bones of time, those years and years and years that separate me from the fucked-up, idealistic, libidinal twenty-six-year-old who moved to San Francisco with nothing but two white hard-sided Samsonite suitcases her parents gave her as a high school graduation gift. I must have brought some books as well because I still own a few I cherished in my teens, the catalogue I bought at the *Dada, Surrealism and Their Heritage* exhibit when it traveled to the Art Institute of Chicago in 1968, an anthology of French poetry, *A Controversy of Poets*. It is impossible for me to look in the mirror and not cringe—which is contrary to so many layers of belief and principles that I hold dear. I believe I should accept myself as I am. I believe that all bodies are valid. My cringe makes me a phony. My chiropractor tells me the muscle in my left hip is atrophying and that I will need a hip replacement unless I start getting down on the floor on all fours and lift my left leg up and back in a kicking motion like a horse kicking away the past that trails behind me. With my super-aging-vison I see what was before hidden, see connections that before were unconnected. In *Anthem* the crones sing: *Distance makes everything seem small.*

In her sixties, Margaret Tedesco looks fantastic—bright eyes, taut skin over chiseled cheekbones and jaw, ice-white bob. Her mother looked young well into advanced age, and then one day her face fell, and she was an old woman. Margaret keeps looking at herself in the mirror, waiting for her fall to happen. She tells me this with an energetic curiosity rather than dread. The flesh holds histories. "Let It Go" moves from past to present. The woman has a terrible secret: *Don't let them know.* In the next line, without transition, the secret's been revealed: *Well now they know.* So fuck it. *Here I stand in the light of day.* Once a woman enters her thirties, her age becomes shameful, and it is impolite to ask it. Many male friends had sixtieth birthday parties, celebrating their triumph over mortality. Especially gay friends—back in the '80s and '90s an epidemic of them didn't make it. But when six-oh happened to me, I swore Kevin to secrecy. That year or maybe the next, Marcella, Liz, and Kristina threw me a birthday party, and them too I swore to secrecy. The only person I remember telling is Ariana Reines. When I moaned that I didn't have much time left, that I was bound to die soon, Ariana said I could have another good thirty years, and I saw this long road ahead of me with a bright light at the end. Thank you, Ariana, for giving me that. There's a freedom in getting caught, in giving up the struggle, in confessing. *Here I stand in the light of day.* I just turned sixty-seven. There. What would friends students acquaintances the checker at Rainbow Grocery do, privy to this ghastly knowledge? I imagine myself thrust behind a giant wall of glass or ice, a thick wall, like those glass bathroom bricks where the world on the other side, though still visible, is distorted—abstracted colored blobs who stretch out, undulate, and stage-whisper, "Sixty-seven!" And I shout back, "Let me out of here! Age is not contagious!" But maybe it is. With each passing year, mortality is normalized— unlike the tragic violation of the AIDS days—the inescapable walks beside me always, like an (un)imaginary friend. Here I stand, sixty-seven—deal with my falling breasts ass biceps neck chances for survival. Let it go. Life flows off of me like a melting ice floe. Is this how Agnès Varda feels now? Michèle Lamy? In her final decades how did Leonora Carrington feel, as she was melting away? Maya Angelou tells Oprah that aging is a gift—think of all the people who didn't make it. God has put a rainbow in the clouds, so whatever hits, Angelou thanks God. "Thank you I'm breathing, Lord."

The Hearing Trumpet: We seemed inspired by some marvellous power, which poured energy into our decrepit carcasses.

Kevin urges me to wear makeup because he says it makes me look like I care. The problem is, I'm not sure I do care. A woman who ages well spends time on her appearance in order to project inner beauty, highlighting her facial features without overdoing it. She moisturizes and exfoliates. She chooses colors that are right for her skin tone, compensating for pallidness with a foundation in a slightly warmer tone. Her eyebrows perfectly frame her face, and pink-toned blush is swirled on the apples of her cheeks. She puts on lipstick with a brush to minimize bleeding. Sheer tangerine lipstick makes her look alive. To combat her jowly jawline, she draws attention to her eyes. She uses a liquid eyeliner that won't pull at her crinkly skin. Her lashes are awakened with an eyelash curler. A highlighter pen applied to cheekbones and brow bone instantly brightens her face. But I see myself aging more like Doris Lessing—large, frail, ancient in mismatched prints and long red scarf, lumbering out of a taxi as reporters inform her she's just won the Nobel Prize, and her not giving a shit. "Oh, Christ!" she exclaims. "It's been going on now for thirty years." Beside her, her larval son Peter, with his arm in a sling, holds a bag of onions and a giant artichoke. "One can't get more excited than one gets, you know."

In the final month of her life, I accompanied my mother to the doctor for a test or some failed procedure to help her breathe better. Sitting on the examination table, she removed a giant underwire bra that her breasts were swimming in. She said she didn't try it on before she bought it, just got the same size she always wore. With her right hand she flopped one of her flaccid breasts up and down and said, "At this point there ain't nothing left but skin." Selfishly I looked at the flesh hanging from her bones and thought in horror, That body will be my body. And then the doctor came in. Mortality, that thug, slams my face against the window, the wall, the steering wheel, leaving me bruised and bloodied, and then there's the big cover-up. Mortality pierces my heart with a slice of ice, and only love can save me. Whose love? When I think of my own aging, I feel remarkably unoriginal. With AIDS, mortality was a freakish invader, but now it's just momentum.

An hourglass figure = a figure whose time is running out.

In the Kingdom of Ice-olation you spit water into the dead seal's mouth so the dead seal will tell its brothers about the nice drink you gave it, and they will come to you, unafraid, and you can kill them more easily. If your baby is a boy, you lick him all over and rub his body with whale blubber. If your baby is a girl, you put her on the ice and fill her mouth with snow. There is no place for too many useless mouths. If you're an old woman with teeth too worn to soften hides, you must be left to die. You cannot change the harsh laws of the people, laws dictated by the harshness of the climate. Sitting alone on the ice on a small piece of fur, wind whooshing all around, you accept without bitterness nature's eternal tragedy, that flesh must perish so that the flesh may live. In the Kingdom of Ice-olation, "to fuck" and "to laugh" are the same word.

The Great Mother never locked the vulnerable away in institutions, nor did she set them out to die. In order to save the world, she must be lured back.

On YouTube, covers of "Let It Go" are endless—grade-schoolers; teens; men; cartoon characters; choirs; violin, keyboard, and recorder solos; punk versions; metal versions; women of all ages singing in all languages, including Latin and Gollum; a cat version; a singing chicken; an African tribal version; trumpet; ukulele; sax; screamo; soul; ASL; chipmunks. *My soul is spiraling in frozen fractals all around.* Fractals are created by repeating a simple process over and over in an ongoing feedback loop. There is not one "Let It Go" but a flurry of them, a never-ending pattern that flutters across the internet. Distortions of the official Disney video are particularly popular with viewers. Each time Elsa sings, "Let it go," the video gets more distorted and the bass increases. Every "Let it go" makes the pitch lower by two semitones and the screen gets fatter. Every time Elsa sings, "Let it go," another silly effect is added. Whenever she sings, "Let it go," it gets higher and brighter. And then there's the masterful sound effects of "Let Your Fart Go," with its 1.5 million views. People love the return of the repressed. Elsa's groomed distress breaks through to uncontainable rage, ballooning her face, melting a meticulously rendered world, turning her words to mush, to groans, screeches, and farts. A viewer comments, "Damn she thicc."

In many cultures old people beyond use value have been mythically or actually put to death. The Heruli, a Germanic tribe (400 to 800 CE), placed the elderly on a tall stack of wood and stabbed them to death before setting the pyre alight. In ancient Japan, elderly relatives were left to die on a mountain or some other desolate locale. Nordic folklore depicts elderly people leaping, or being thrown, to their deaths. "Ättestupa," the Swedish term for this practice, has been reintroduced in modern political contexts as a metaphor for the horrors of underfunded social services, especially for retirees. Serbians used an axe or stick to terminate the useless, and the entire village was invited to attend. The family placed corn mush on the head of the victim in order to finger the corn as the killer, instead of themselves. Among the Inuit, senicide was rare, except during times of famine. No case of an Inuit senicide has been documented since 1939. According to the internet, because of capitalism, "Eskimos are no longer in an environment in which their survival is on the line." To this day, in Tamil Nadu, a state of India, family members practice an elaborate euthanasia ritual—after a morning oil bath, the elderly relative is given enough coconut water to cause an overdose, complete with renal failure, high fever, and fits. This occurs dozens—or even hundreds—of times a year. In the United States, where health care is in crisis, the elderly are abandoned in public places or outside hospital emergency rooms. This phenomenon, known as "granny dumping," peaks over Christmas holidays. It is estimated that American families ditch up to 70,000 elderly relatives per year.

The woman who ages well eats sensibly small amounts to compensate for a lowered metabolism. She focuses on oats, oranges, avocados, brussels sprouts, salmon, grapes, dark chocolate, and a single glass of red wine per day. She stretches and does weight-bearing exercises but not the wrong ones, which could fracture her spine. She keeps her hair shoulder-length or shorter. She's had a professional bra fitting to keep the girls upright. She has rediscovered how to play, and creativity is her primary goal. She combines the fruits of maturity with childlike wonder. She favors natural fabrics—cotton, linen, silk—and is skilled at accessorizing. She makes the most of her new body shape, her new face shape, through the subtle art of camouflage. She wears body-skimming, not baggy, clothes. Layering works wonders, particularly solid-colored single-breasted open jackets with small lapels. When she looks in the mirror in Berkeley, she says, "Yes, I am pleased with myself." She takes her place beside Anne Walsh, whips her arms around to mimic a storm, makes whooshing sounds, and sings, *The cold never bothered me anyway.*

11

The Ghosts We Live With

Most ghosts are confused. They manifest pale and elongated. But some ghosts are professionals, spirits who use a medium to enter a circle of believers. They plunge their disembodied arms into hot wax, and the wax hardens to a hollow skin, capturing the shape of a thumb from beyond or a clawlike fist. Believers display these bits of dimensionality in glass-fronted cabinets. Ghosts flow through key holes, flicker behind the bathroom door while you splash in the tub. Ghosts sneak up from behind when you look in a mirror, where in its gloss you too waver about, flat and empty. Some ghosts have personalities and can even speak. They convey their emotions via smells the living recognize. Other ghosts manifest as vaporous fogs or cold swirling funnels. Some are fragments of disembodied drives, little glowing orbs that that zip about super fast.

An evolved ghost is called an entity. An entity knows what it wants and who to terrorize to get it. Flashes of a bramble-headed woman appear at the foot of your bed. Poltergeist means noisy ghost because it bangs things around. It lives inside your TV and rearranges the objects in your home in configurations that break the laws of gravity. At first you find its quirkiness charming, but eventually it slams you against the wall, hangs your body upside-down from the ceiling like a bat. You wake up in the middle of fucking and find yourself alone in bed, pummeled by this energy envelope that smells like rancid wax. Ghosts slain in battle are particularly persistent. To escape them, you must run around your village three times and wash yourself.

My building predates the 1906 earthquake, a humble Victorian built for workers. Its embossed walls are thick with residual ectoplasm from all the lives that have passed through these six units. We host a hungry ghost who moves from apartment to apartment, latching onto holes in the occupant's aura, forcing them to overindulge in alcohol drugs food or sex. The preppy guy in 18A is suddenly a major stoner, pasty with zits on his face. The guy next door with the wealthy Republican parents goes from being a responsible citizen to a drunk who plays video games full volume, at all hours, explosions of guns and bombs rattling our shared living room wall. His family ships him back to Vermont for detox. His replacement is a drunk from the get-go, abandoning the apartment to druggy friends. I peek through their open front door and see a maze of filth, like the contents of more than one apartment have fused and are stacked in a double layer. The handsome rocker guy I've lived above for years suddenly becomes a junkie. When his drugs are delivered, I see him in front of our building, in sweatpants, shaky and thin, walking with a cane, sucking a red white and blue rocket-shaped popsicle. He stops paying rent, is evicted, and his friends ship him back to LA for detox. After he leaves, I feel this presence wavering in the doorway, waiting. I start eating like there is no tomorrow, and now I'm fat because of the Minna Street ghost.

My back porch office starts to rock and shake, making me queasy. It's not an earthquake. It's not a poltergeist. It's the alcoholic skateboarder who's moved in, a foot and a half beneath my floorboards, fucking in his illegal loft bed. Demons are making him fuck, the same demons that live inside my computer, demons who compel me to binge on information. I press the search button over and over and information streams through my eyes and into my body, so much information it's impossible to retain any particular bit of it. Online information, like avant-garde poetry or music, is a process, an onrush you experience moment by moment by moment, with no catchy tune, no overarching meaning, to pull it all together. It's not substances ghosts are hungry for, but time—a metronomic immersion to break the vast gray vague of eternity. Out of glowing screens they reach, lusting for time.

WHERE

12

On Becoming Undone

I first encountered the Sumerian myth of Inanna in the 1980s, when I read Sylvia Brinton Perera's *Descent to the Goddess: A Way of Initiation for Women* (1981). At the time I was plagued with a neurological disorder in which electrified waves would shoot through my body, distorting my sensory processing in ways that terrified me. I memorized Sylvia Plath's "The Hanging Man": *By the roots of my hair some god got hold of me./ I sizzled in his blue volts like a desert prophet.* What if these blue volts went on forever, I fretted—what if the world as I knew it was over? When Inanna enters the underworld she is stripped of everything—clothing, crown, jewels, personality. She is reduced to a slab of rotting meat, hung on the wall from a hook. Eventually, through the help of trusty allies, Inanna returns. Thus her story gave me great comfort. Perhaps as she did, I too would someday reenter the land of the living.

I had signed up for an online, eight-hour solstice ritual, tracking Inanna's journey through the underworld. On the winter solstice, the longest night of the year, devotees light fires to encourage the sun's return. A week before, a chronic condition I've been in denial about turned acute, and I decided I was too weak to handle the Inanna ceremony. I scheduled an endoscopy instead.

For that, my weakness worked in my favor. Normally, for any medical procedure—a dental cleaning, even—I'm like a neurotic, yapping poodle. But for this, I am resigned, pliable.

A short, squat, grandmotherly woman who uses few words instructs me to remove my jewelry and all clothing except my panties. Then she gives me a gown patterned with the hospital's logo ("fasten it in the back") and a pair of slipper socks. I'm allowed to keep my glasses so I can read the consent form—the third one of the afternoon I'm required to sign. She fastens an identification band around my wrist and has me lie down with my hands wrapped in warm towels. "To make your veins big." She reminds me of a character from *Game of Thrones*. She is so gruff and a bit feral—but also calming, like she's seen it all. There is quite a class hierarchy among the nursing staff. She is clearly on a lower rung, compared to the Noel Cowardish sophisticated nurses who will assist the gastroenterologist. This woman is more my class. Like her, I am blunt and feral. She sticks a port into my hand and it hurts like hell. I am hooked up to saline solution. No longer do I have knowledge of what will enter my body.

Just last night, at a "Jewish Christmas" party, I was drinking official *Game of Thrones* wine with writer and curator Gravity Goldberg. From the wine's website: "This blend of select lots is considered among the finest in the Seven Kingdoms by those who prefer dry, robust reds." I tentatively took a sip and said it tasted smoky. "With lots of cherry," Gravity added, and the taste of cherry burst forth into my mouth. Since I'd recently been to Berlin, and Gravity works for San Francisco's Contemporary Jewish Museum, the conversation turned to the Holocaust, to the question of remembering versus moving on. Gravity said that much of her job is deciding how much to remember the Holocaust. In the US, if the past were honored, we'd live in a much less fucked-up situation than the one in which we find ourselves. A dog walked past us in the crowded kitchen. Gravity raised her glass: "Here's to the dire wolf."

I am wheeled away to the procedure room where oxygen is fastened to my nose, and a blood pressure cuff is attached to my left arm. As I lie on my left side, a donut-shaped thing is inserted into my mouth. This is surprisingly comfortable, so they must have already started drugging me. My mouth is round and no longer can I speak. Like Inanna, I am a blob of flesh at their mercy. I remember seeing bands of deep color—and belching sounds. Whenever there's a belching I see a band of black. Undifferentiated, preverbal expulsion, my propped-open mouth circular as a Cheerio. I am no longer a person. I am a system of inhalation and evacuation.

When I visited my mother during the last few years of her life, when she was a widow with lung cancer, in the middle of the night she would emit these moans and wails that didn't sound human—but more like sheer animal terror—like she had reached this place where no sentient being could bear to be. Is there tenderness at the end of our undoing? I hope so.

And then the endoscopy's over and I ask one of the glamorous nurses what was that belching sound, and she says they were pumping air into me. And then I'm lying in the original place where I stripped away, and there's a new nurse, a young guy—the blood pressure cuff is still tightening intermittently, and other things are being monitored so something must be attached to a finger somewhere. Eventually the guy nurse gives me a paper cup of ice water, which I sip greedily and then the doctor appears and tells me stuff I pretty much can take in. Then Kevin arrives and more water and cranberry juice, as reality gradually sharpens. I get dressed and Kevin is given written instructions. I'm wearing my wristband, there's a bandage on my right hand, and I walk carefully, holding on to Kevin because the nurses warned me about falling down. I feel shaky but calm, and my self has softly returned; yet there's a sense of peering out into the world rather than existing in it.

For Christmas, Kevin drove me to a particularly scenic stretch of coast known as Lands End. On a beautiful, bright day, we walked along the wet sand amongst frolicking lovers, families, dogs, and sporty types who looked perfectly comfortable in bare feet and hooded sweatshirts, while the rest of us huddled in down. As the afternoon wore on, the sun slowly sank in the sky, and I recited from Plath's "Finisterre": *This was the land's end: the last fingers, knuckled and rheumatic,/ Cramped on nothing.* When the sun neared the horizon, all activity stopped, and we all faced the shore in rapt attention—perhaps with mounting anxiety?—as the sun continued to drop, slipping into the Pacific, disappearing. Except for the waves and the shrieking of birds—nature sounds—the beach was totally silent. It was like each of us had hooked into some ancient part of our DNA. The sun has died and night is upon us. What rituals need we perform to rebirth the sun? What rituals need we perform to keep our myths and histories alive?

13

Photo Op

I flash my SFMOMA lifetime artist membership card, and the woman at the counter asks me, "What do you have in the collection?" Her question gets me tense. A few months after the museum sent me the card in the mail—a total surprise—some brainiac in acquisitions questioned my eligibility, and they threatened to revoke my membership. See me on the phone, shouting at a museum bureaucrat, "You've got to be kidding me! This is beyond tacky." So this cheerful woman at the counter—I do not know if she's just being chatty or if this is a test. I say my husband has a piece in the Kikibox. She looks confused and asks, "What's that?" I answer, "There was a gallery here in the '90s and they made a box with stuff in it." I grab my ticket and scurry over to the stairs that lead to the show "snap + share: transmitting photographs from mail art to social networks."

Kiki was a seminal gallery that exhibited in San Francisco's Mission district from 1993–95. After 15 months it closed, due to the failing health of curator Rick Jacobsen, who died of AIDS in February 1997. The Kikibox, produced in 1994, was a collection of unique items made by artists involved with the gallery. My husband, Kevin Killian, wrote out by hand "Three on a Match," a poet's theater production he put on at Kiki; one page included in each Kikibox. Kiki was so small, there was no room for the actors when they weren't performing. So they had to stand outside on the street with their ears to the door, and when it was time for them to enter, they would open the front door and walk on "stage," then go back outside when they finished their lines. I'm not in the Kikibox, but I did write a piece for the chapbook Rick made in conjunction with his Yoko Ono tribute show. Yoko heard about the show, and she left one of her signature screams on the gallery's message machine.

"Snap + Share," organized by Clément Chéroux, the museum's senior photography curator, centers, like the Kikibox, on the distribution of the ephemeral—postcards, snapshots, pinhole cameras that capture their journey as they move through the mail, and the deluge of digital images uploaded to the beyond of social media. Included are pieces by established artists such as Moyra Davey, Lynn Hershman Leeson, Ray Johnson, but many of the works are by amateurs, their rationale for being displayed in an art museum as shaky as my being granted a lifetime artist's membership.

While much has been written accusing the internet of destroying photography as an art form, "Snap + Share" celebrates recent paradigm shifts. The show's core premise is that no longer is the dissemination of a photograph subordinate to its production, but a defining element in the photographic process. Furthermore, photography has transcended mere image-making to become a language in itself. To illustrate this point, in his introduction to the show's catalogue, Chéroux quotes Evan Spiegel, the founder of Snapchat: "People wonder why their daughter is taking ten thousand photos a day. What they don't realize is that she isn't preserving images. She's talking." A pouting selfie is worth a thousand words.

The following night I find myself sleeping in a hospital room in an armchair that folds out into a cot, in front of a window. The condition of the patient I'm visiting is serious; terrifying actually. I'm determined not to take any photos, to not be so tasteless. The memories that are being created here, I want to erase, not freeze. We'll ultimately spend eleven nights in the hospital, long enough that the experience becomes normalized. Medical types wake up the patient at all hours, poking and performing procedures. Nurses bring us endless pitchers of ice water and, if we ask nicely, little cardboard cups of ice cream, chocolate for the patient, vanilla for me. Curator Liz Thomas visits, and on the flat screen hanging from the wall, the three of us watch Melissa McCarthy in *Life of the Party,* which I've already seen on a plane. Liz and I covertly sip from cans of hard cider, not sure if we are doing something forbidden. After the movie, Liz notices the swirly, highly photoshopped, abstract flower image hanging on the wall behind the patient. "What's the point of that?" Liz muses. The patient can't see it, so why is it there—other than to serve as a background for photos?

Subsequently, as I walk through the hospital corridors I notice similar flower patterns crowning the headboard of every bed, with more elaborate arrangements swooshing vividly across the translucent screen on each floor that separates the bank of elevators from the visitors' lounge. The designs are seductive, beseeching me to throw myself or someone else in front of them and snap away. But I resist. Then one night at 2:30 in the morning, I get up to pee, and when I return to my cot, I notice on the roof of the empty parking garage across the street a guy working on a bicycle that has been turned upside-down. In the stark lighting, suspended above near-featureless concrete, the bike's spokey wheels turn carnivalesque. Hunched over in his black hoodie, the guy looks like an troll who has stepped out of another dimension. Above the bike's seat a red light flashes incessantly.

Hanging over the back of my fold-out chair-bed, pushing my iPhone 6S's camera to the limit—low light, zooming on an object in the distance—I snap eighteen photos, hoping one will turn out right. The photo bug has infected me, and after that I cannot stop. I turn around and capture the privacy curtain, which in the darkened room glows with light that seeps in from the hallway. The next day, when the patient leaves for an MRI, I photograph his floral headboard decor. Then the bouquet that sits on a ledge as Wendy Williams emotes on the flat screen. I do not photograph the patient. It is safe to document the staging, but not the play. Later, when curator Anthony Huberman brings us lunch, I position him in front of the privacy curtain, and say, "This is the perfect backdrop, Anthony." Anthony flashes a smile as if he were posing for a Scene and Heard diary, our hospital room a glamorous hot spot.

If photography has become a language, what are my photos saying? I'm not totally sure, for in all communication there is a surplus beyond one's intent. Perhaps the images assert that even in the midst of institutionalized crisis there is pleasure and connection, and times when space crystalizes in such a manner that you stop everything—you cannot help yourself—and you stare and snap.

14

Kevin and Dodie

with Kevin Killian

> *"I know the butterfly is my soul grown weak from battle."*
> — John Wieners

Week 1, April 28, 2019
Origins (Dodie)

Dodie Bellamy: So, here are the parameters of this project, which I proposed to you. We will aim for a target of 1,000 words a week, for a year. If we go over that, fine, but 1,000 is enough. Each week will have a topic, which we will take turns choosing. Whoever chooses the topic, begins the dialogue. There are no limitations as far as topics go. They can include the present, the past, gossip, ideas, art, etc. This week I chose "Origin"—the history of our endeavors to write a book together.

Kevin Killian: This is an amazing update of a project we began—and failed at—I don't know how long ago. Fifteen years? No, longer. I know! It was the week Wieners died. March, 2002. We had proposed what seemed like a great idea to Lyn Hejinian and Travis Ortiz to write a volume for their newly launched press, Atelos. Everybody else was going to write poetry or theory, but you and I had been on the scene here in San Francisco for so long that we would just tell our memories of the things we had seen. We had the perfect title, *Eyewitness*.

DB: And then we tried a sample chapter, of our memories of John Wieners, who had just died. You're an avid collaborator, while I'm such a control freak; the process has never appealed to me that much. It seems to me that whenever you collaborate, the result sounds like a piece by Kevin Killian, and my ego is too big for that. Though I've enjoyed writing copy with you for flyers and things like that. When I was the director of Small Press Traffic in the '90s I remember us having a great time writing crazy copy for the flyers and reviews. And I got so good at your style that some of the most Kevin-esque passages were actually me doing a pastiche of you. So, we got through like a paragraph on Wieners, and the project became this object of discussion that never materialized—like George and Martha's phantom child in Edward Albee's *Who's Afraid of Virginia Woolf?*

KK: It was a disaster. It underlined totally how little we think alike and how differently we remembered basically the same events. It was so painful writing that one page that we never worked together again until we re-began work on our anthology of New Narrative writing. I remembered that we went on a cruise with John Wieners to get some "digestive aids" in North Beach on the rare occasion of his 1990 return to San Francisco, after decades away. I think you and I still have a package of those "digestive aids" he was hunting for, which turned out to be a package of Life Savers candy. You could have bought it anywhere but he wanted to go to one store.

DB: So, already I disagree with a few things you've said. In my memory, Lynn asked us to write a joint book, and our memoir was what we came up with. I remember going around dramatically telling people that everybody else got their own Atelos book, but I had to share mine with you, like I was just half a writer. Meanwhile, Rae Armantrout had her own book. Pamela Lu had her own book, Leslie Scalapino had her own book, and on and on.

The Wieners Life Savers were multicolored. He bought a tube for each of us, and one of us ate their tube and one of us—probably you with your archival fever—saved their tube and eventually sent it with our archives to Yale. In my memory, we were walking through Chinatown with Wieners and Raymond Foye, either before or after we went for drinks at Tosca—and Wieners walked into a random store and bought the "aids." These details are minor, but in a conventional collaboration, what do you do with them other than fight with one another over stupid stuff.

KK: What I remember is in the years in which I stored Wieners' Life Savers in your dentist cabinet, and I'd open the drawer, looking for a pair of scissors or whatever, is that Life Savers go rotten. The package itself looked kind of dusty/dirty, melted, and every time I noticed this deterioration it reinforced in me the idea that you and I should never write together.

I also am thinking now that when he was hunting for digestive aids, it was the height of the AIDS epidemic.

DB: His conversation, both at his reading for the SF State Poetry Center, and in private conversation, was highly coded, so your AIDS connection may be spot on.

KK: You and I and Raymond were racing after Wieners, who was leading us in a heraldic quest to save our lives, like the White Knight in *Alice in Wonderland*.

DB: So you don't think our talking here about candy is juvenile?

KK: Add into this, also, the fact that in the legend of Hart Crane he was a rich man's son whose father had become wealthy from controlling the rights to Life Savers, and in many ways Wieners saw himself as the son of Crane.

In our case, candy is not only a metaphor, but one piece of solid evidence that the entirety of our interchange with John Wieners happened, and that you and I still had no way of describing our separate encounters with Wieners' genius, how he, among all poets of his generation, affected each of us deeply, but in very different ways. In a way, we had each come separately to San Francisco to meet him. And working with him and Raymond for a close period was one of the defining moments of our lives as artists.

DB: So maybe that's why we're still together. I'm totally behind you on what you say about Wieners' genius, and, yes, he's had an enormous impact on my writing. When I wrote that piece dedicated for him, "Not Clinical But Probable," which was published in *City Lights Review*, I heard that at his own reading at the Poetry Project, Wieners read from my piece. And then there's the whole issue that since there was all this sex with schizophrenic poets in the piece, the rumors were flying that I'd had an affair with Wieners, as if one homosexual poet—you—weren't enough for me.

KK: Thus are legends born. But to write a book of our memories seemed like it was asking for trouble and so we closed the page for twenty years. But then, in 2017, the artist Ugo Rondinone asked that we write a catalogue essay for his show at the Berkeley Art Museum—his first show in the Bay Area—"*the world just makes me laugh*." Ugo instructed us to tape a candid conversation as we walked through the objects in the show.

DB: We did visit the show together and had a wonderful afternoon, but being writers, we faked the conversation. There was no taping. We just sat down at the computer and began our back and forth. And it was so pleasurable and effortless, and exciting. Mostly because we didn't have to agree on anything. Ugo said it would be interesting to hear our conflicting points of view, rather than a unified front.

KK: Maybe it was easy because Ugo's show was all about clowns. Clowns are amusing, childish, grotesque. They're not a subject to be taken seriously. And yet, his treatment of this theatrical subject invited our own associations, not only of clowns we'd seen as kids, but as a subject for fine art over several centuries.

DB: That tension between wanting to risk foolishness, yet wanting to be taken seriously seems to me central to both of our writing practices. Happily, both artist and curator (Larry Rinder) approved of our text, and asked for very few changes. So, a few weeks ago when we were again asked to write a joint catalogue essay (and the fact that anybody would want us to write a joint catalogue essay confuses me) for the Mike Kelley show that was recently at 500 Capp Street—*Mike Kelley: Pushing and Pulling, Pulling and Pushing*" (November 3, 2018–February 16, 2019)— you proposed another dialogue. And it was equally pleasurable to work on.

KK: Actually, the Capp Street curators wanted either of us or both, but I was incapable at that time of writing anything about Mike Kelley without your help because of my medical problems, so I needed you as never before, and you gave everything. In both these cases it was fun because Ugo and Mike are among the favorite artists of both of us, which is weird because we don't agree on many things.

DB: And then I got the idea for this book and bugged the shit out of you until you agreed. Why did you finally cave in?

KK: The horror of the one paragraph of *Eyewitness* that we wrote was pleasantly balanced out by the great reception we've had for our anthology, *Writers Who Love Too Much: New Narrative 1977–1997*. Remember, that was a project posing many more dangers to our marriage than *Eyewitness*.

DB: But on the critical parts of the book, we didn't totally collaborate. You'd write, I'd read and give suggestions, and you'd write more. I feel like I was more of a developmental editor for that book. My input is integral, but I let you lead on the writing. And here we're going to try to perform as equals. For one year.

KK: I feel like opening that dentist drawer one more time and looking at that candy. But it's gone.

Week 2, May 5, 2019
Communal Presence: New Narrative Writing Today (Kevin)

KK: I remember the excitement and the dread of the New Narrative conference at UC Berkeley in the fall of 2017, which followed the publication of our *Writers Who Love Too Much*, and Rob Halpern and Robin Tremblay-McGaw's *From Our Hearts to Yours: New Narrative as Contemporary Practice*. Two branches of Cal (Berkeley and Santa Cruz) were joining forces and actually doing this. Ten years before, I don't think anybody thought of New Narrative as anything other than a failed experiment or, at best, a forgotten avant-garde.

DB: I don't agree that New Narrative was forgotten. There's been a history of younger poets taking it up, such as Dana Ward, and pushing its concepts into new directions, sometimes more poetic than what early practitioners worked in, even though the movement was founded by poets who didn't know how to write narrative. I remember asking Bob about some stupid formalist issue about "craft" my fiction students brought up that I found oppressive, and Bob had never heard of it, though it was commonly taught in fiction workshops. And he seemed blessed to me, not having the burden of such toxic exposure. Until recently most of our invites to universities have been generated by grad students (rather than faculty), and the *Communal Presence* conference continued that trend.

KK: The coolest part is that we got to stay on campus at the Women's Faculty Club, a classic Julia Morgan building, teetering between mansion and dump, tucked into a corner of the campus few people knew about.

DB: It was next to Optometry or something.

KK: There we stayed, as if in a dorm, with the world's oldest students—Eileen Myles, Dennis Cooper, Nayland Blake, Carla Harryman, and on and on. So many friends, some of whom we'd grown apart from somewhat. We were reunited at last like one of those '80s movies like *The Big Chill*, eating breakfast together, and it was in the middle of a horrible firestorm in Napa, and many wore surgical masks.

DB: The organizers did not intend to house locals at the Women's Faculty Club. We were only there because I threw a "diva" when I found out our panel was scheduled for 9 am, saying I couldn't possibly get from San Francisco to Berkeley that early. So their compromise was to give us a room and change our panel to 11. And so we're in Berkeley in the middle of all this smoke, which was milder in San Francisco, and I was missing the pricey air filters I have in our apartment, and it seemed like karma paying me back for being such a bitch.

KK: To an astonishing degree, organizers Eric Sneathen and Daniel Benjamin followed our roadmap of who we wanted to share the stage with us. Not necessarily the most famous writers, but those our anthology insists are vital. Gabrielle Daniels, Michael Amnasan, Roberto Bedoya. Confounding everybody, we persuaded Judy Grahn to come—not a New Narrative writer herself, but a forebear.

DB: Judy Grahn's reading of her epic 1974 poem "A Woman is Talking to Death," in the Maude Fife room at Wheeler Hall, was one of the most powerful readings I've ever seen. People were stunned, brought to tears, hanging on every word. When she finished, I left the room and sat by myself in the lounge because nothing could follow that.

KK: She seemed to lose strength around part seven of the nine parts, like she was going to faint, and kept herself going through sheer force of will, but eventually her partner, Kris Brandenburger, helped her to her seat and finished the reading for her. Presently Grahn rose, gave a weak wave, and faced an insane crowd that had been driven mad by ecstasy, the spectacle of her dying and coming back to life in front of our eyes, I guess kind of an allegory for New Narrative itself in this context.

DB: I feel low grade panic at all conferences, but at this one there were so many people I had complex histories with that needed to be negotiated, plus a couple of years before that I'd had the experience of being shunned and bullied by a group of East Bay poets, so I tend to avoid East Bay poetry events. I pretty much tried to erase myself from the whole conference. The big reading event with all us oldsters took place at the Omni Commons, which had been a focal space for the bullies. I gave a short, uninspired reading because I just didn't want to be up there. Despite my discomfort—and that godawful smoke—I found the weekend to be tender, with many cherished bits of conversation, and then there was that one panel I attended where one of the young women presenting kept mouthing to me across the room, "I love you."

KK: Then there was the drama of the bedbugs in our fabulous Julia Morgan residence. I think only Nayland got them bad and had to change rooms. There was something biblical, though, about the smoke and the pests, something from Leviticus. It was really like the end of the world. I remember introducing Nayland to Renee Gladman, who, remarkably, had never met. It was two eras colliding, finding a common space, a communal presence, I guess.

I understand, Dodie, that you were uncomfortable about the complexities of all the social interactions, and, indeed, what was happening in the outside world in that moment, basically the rise of Trump. My reactions were a little different, just a tide of disbelief that this was really happening, that hundreds of people came. Not just scholars, but artists and musicians, filmmakers. Corin Sworn was there, do you remember Dodie, all the way from Glasgow?

DB: No, I don't remember Corin being there, but when we got to know her a bit in Glasgow and she was so great, I felt I'd missed a chance in Berkeley, and I wondered how many other chances I let slip through my fingers due to my social whatevers.

KK: I want to talk about the hierarchy of the conference, how one evening we drove the estimable Brian Blanchfield back to where he was staying, and it was this crummy little hotel, way down University, halfway to the freeway, and how this reflected something of a caste system I will never understand. I mean caste system of academia.

DB: I get what you're saying in principle. Being an adjunct I live and breathe from a lower rung in such a system, but we were the subjects of the conference, so it makes sense we'd be treated differently. But, it's odd to be both subject and participant in something at the same time. Like who are you? And the conference seemed to invite a sort of egomania that I think most of us were trying our best to resist. Not all, but most.

KK: And then there was the spectacle of Bruce Boone wearing lavish, blue eye shadow during his reading at the Omni. It was like what the hell. It was like a declaration from Bruce, yes you haven't heard much from me for decades, but I am back, and I am a classic legend.

DB: Many of us had felt ourselves part of New Narrative—but had grown out of it. Michael Amnasan, though he's kept on writing, had cut off almost all contacts with a literary community. He wouldn't even answer our emails when we asked him to be in our anthology. Somehow I found out his wife was a New York-based food blogger, so I looked up her blog, and left a plea for Michael to contact us in the comments section of one of her blog posts. That worked.

But, anyway, there was an off-kilter feeling of being on the outskirts of a moment for years, and then suddenly finding oneself sucked back into the center. Though "finding" is not really an accurate verb, since we edited an entire anthology promoting the subject. Like all the fairy tales warn, be careful what you wish for.

KK: And everywhere the ghosts of people who did not live to see this conference.

DB: That's the one thing I asked for that Daniel and Eric did not provide—some sort of panel or reading or remembrance for people involved with New Narrative who had died. Sam D'Allesandro, Bob Flanagan, Lawrence Braithwaite, Steve Abbott, Marsha Campbell, John Norton. Of course, some of these people were discussed in panels. Our ghosts.

KK: Ghosts in the smoke.

Week 3, May 16, 2019
Mortality (Dodie)

DB: I was planning to suggest a more fun topic, but after the last few days—the death of the artist Lutz Bacher and our visit this morning to the weird oncologist, there would be this huge elephant in the room of any other topic besides mortality. Are you okay talking about that?

KK: Not to mention the way the week started off, with the death of Peggy Lipton, whom I loved so much?

DB: Was she on *Mod Squad*?

KK: Yes, she was the one from *Mod Squad*, in the '70s, I guess. Julie. And, also to top it off, as if though Peggy Lipton's death wasn't enough, Doris Day died within 24 hours. Funny thing is, Doris also played in a movie called *Julie*. She was a stewardess with an abusive husband she was trying to escape. Louis Jourdan. He terrorized her on an airplane. People think of Doris as some kind of sexy virgin, trying to preserve her virginity, but she was often tormented and abused by the men in her life.

The other point about Peggy Lipton and Doris Day, blonde American girls next door, is that they were race pioneers. Peggy shocked the world when she married the musician Quincy Jones, and Doris—much much older and considered something of a square in the music world—allowed herself to be photographed behind a piano singing with Sly Stone in the pages of *Rolling Stone*. They were both dangerous women, or women dangerous to patriarchy.

Then there was Lutz Bacher. And then a simple phone call from Andrew Durbin made it clear that the world of death had come awfully close.

DB: Today you made jokes about what bad taste it was for Andrew to ask you, with your cancer diagnosis, to write an obituary as your entrance into *Frieze*. Did writing and thinking about Lutz highlight your own mortality, or did the process of pushing around words shield you from that?

Reading your piece made me long for the '90s San Francisco art scene, in a sort of tragic way. For me, even the fondest of memories are laden with a sort of death. The finality of their past tense, and my rewriting them in my memory. Your quoting a passage I wrote about Lutz, detailing something I had no active memory of. Even now, it's all kind of blurry and might as well have been a memory of a movie. Who lived that life? It doesn't quite feel like me.

KK: Out of the *Frieze* obituary I left the most melodramatic story, as any responsible journalist would. As I remember hearing it, Lutz's professor-husband, Donald Backer, retired from UC Berkeley's astronomy department, lost his health benefits and collapsed in 2010 outside their home, and Lutz is said to have blamed the university system for his death. According to Darrell Alvarez, when he and Lutz both had shows at the Berkeley Art Museum in 2012, Lutz never went to see her show, so linked was the university for her with Don's death. She sold her house for under market value, moved to New York, fired her Bay Area gallerist, and, in a spectacularly operatic gesture, never returned. Vengeful, haunted, she lived out the rest of her life in a haze of renunciation. Paradise had been lost. Bitterness took over.

DB: I love your novelization of Lutz's life post-Don, which you're spinning out of very little information. But I suspect you're seeing into some core truth she most likely hid.

KK: Maybe I'm just projecting because that's how I feel right now.

DB: But you've been so happy lately, in your partially steroid-induced bliss. You're not actively expressing these darker emotions. I'm the one in our relationship who holds the dark emotions.

KK: Oh Dodie, you know every year I would write an Oscars column for *Fanzine*, and every year I was bitter, bitter that Doris Day had never won the honorary Oscar. Nobody took Peggy Lipton seriously either, until she returned to TV in middle age in *Twin Peaks*. People stopped laughing at Lutz when she showed emotion—before that she was like a clown, like a Sturtevant without brains, like a pathetic scamp—think of Giuletta Masina or Agnes Varda, sad sacks poking fun at themselves.

DB: Your metaphor is confusing me, because GM and AV sound like they're all about emotion.

KK: They're about downplaying emotion before other people can poke fun of them. And one gesture—all Lutz had to do was raise an arm and point a finger, and she became like Angelina Jolie in *Maleficent*, a terrible, rage-consumed creature seized with power.

DB: And so how are you projecting into all of this?

KK: My cancer diagnosis wouldn't have happened to me if I'd had a better attitude about myself, a more powerful sense of myself. If I had named names instead of shrugging, when bad things happened to you or to me.

But I wanted to return to your lack of memory about your exchanges with Lutz. You didn't even realize she was one of the characters in your novel. You saw stills from her screen tests of you looking as ravishing as any screen goddess, and you said, that can't be me. What is erasure all about? It's not just death, it's . . . forgetting. It's not just forgetting, it's the inability to take in pleasure and a sense of one's own worth.

DB: Are you saying I can't take in pleasure?

KK: It has no permanent resting place in your psyche. But what am I saying, I just ate a whole candy bar, a giant candy bar, shaped like the map of California, like in the Jack Spicer poem "Psychoanalysis: An Elegy" (I want to write a poem as long as California and as slow as a summer), so maybe I'm kind of nuts right now. After going to the Joan Brown show at Anglim Gilbert this afternoon we came home and spent half an hour weeping hopelessly because we were going to miss each other so much if the worst happens. And I said it may not happen for a long time. Both of us have a sense of ending and that's one of our strengths as writers and thinkers.

How long did it take me to imagine the end of *Spreadeagle*? Twenty-three years? How long did it take you to finish *The Letters of Mina Harker*? Fifteen years? Sam D'Allesandro had to die. And when you were writing "In the Shadow of Twitter Towers," you thought it was finished, but nobody had died. Then Omar (the guy whose body was found in a suitcase) died, and your piece went on and on, gaining in power, gaining in horror, until you had set fire to the whole system of the city.

DB: I'm thinking of how Dennis Cooper said AIDS ruined death. It doesn't sound like your cancer diagnosis is ruining death for you, but that it's a generative thing.

KK: You and I lived through AIDS, and during those fifteen years there was literally nothing but hopelessness, nothing but death.

DB: Yes, but despite the grief and the sheer terror—and maybe even because of it—there also was a wonderful sense of community. People didn't have the bandwidth for pettiness. The art scene felt so important, so vital. There was an openness.

KK: I think that there's more hope these days so that there's less community, less art, less operatic passion.

DB: How can you believe that in the Trump era there's more hope? I find myself saying repeatedly, Capitalism is winning, Capitalism will always win. And it doesn't give a damn about us.

KK: Dennis' point is that once we were in love with death in the Punk Era. It seemed like the real thing, the point of living. Then came AIDS, and death was reduced to nothing. Just the end. It was stripped of meaning.

DB: The act of growing old, which seems like such an impossible thing to have happened to me, makes mortality tasteable, like it's on my tongue. At this stage in life, its inevitability is so clear, and there's this constant sense of impending. How has getting ill impacted that sense for you? Is it the same but more heightened? Or is it a new feeling all together? And I imagine this will shift over time, once you're getting treatments, etc.

KK: I think it's all those things. Let's wait a few weeks and see what happens. And, oh, Dodie, I have so much to say still about Peggy Lipton and Doris Day.

Week 4, May 18, 2019
Drawing (Kevin)

KK: I started making poem drawings when we heard that CA Conrad was trying to raise money for Frank Sherlock's hospitalization in Philadelphia around 2005. Frank had come down with encephalitis after spending weeks and months helping the people of New Orleans cope with the devastation of Hurricane Katrina. Or at least that's what we heard.

DB: When we saw him he was frail and walking around with a cane and looked quite noble. People were stunned, and he was heavily romanticized.

KK: His black beard, like a pirate's beard. The beard was alive and so was the cane, but the rest of him was dead. He was a bouncer at a bar called Dirty somebody's. I remember the two of us being there.

DB: Did we go there more than once—because that's the place where I got into the fight with David Buuck, and the two of us stood outside screaming at each other, as the Philadelphia poets stood round, observing. It was similar in a way at the Orono conference on the poetry of the '50s, when Barrett Watten and Marjorie Perloff stood in a communal lounge and shouted into each other's faces about capitalism, and we stood round silently cheering as if at a boxing match. Except, with David and me there were no pretenses of it not being personal. You weren't on the trip, and David was supposed to take care of me, and I didn't think he was doing a good enough job, and every time he'd disappointed me since the mid-'90s came flooding back. Of course after that drama, having released the steam of our tensions, our friendship has been sweet ever since.

KK: Maybe that's how Barrett and Marjorie feel.

DB: I don't think so.

KK: It was Conrad, Frank's best friend, who came up with the idea of getting the poets to write out a poem of their own and then to auction them off on eBay. Which seemed marvelously innovative at the time. This was before Kickstarter. When I saw the names of the other poets I shrank like a butterfly. Conrad has powerful friends. Susan Howe. Dottie Lasky. Colorful people. Like Dottie could bedazzle a poem with fake precious jewels glued to the piece of paper. What could I do? How could I compete? And so I decided to use Sharpies to draw pictures on my poem. I wouldn't type, I would write the words out by hand. Calligraphy.

DB: I might call it anti-calligraphy. I notice that this is like the fourth time in the past few days you've referred to butterflies. Which reminds me of a photo I saw the other day of a woman looking at a display of Nabokov's butterfly collection, which I find kind of creepy. Precise and creepy.

Butterflies are traditionally metaphors for the soul. Is the soul something you've had at the back of your consciousness lately?

KK: I remember going to Santa Cruz with you and stopping at this one grove of trees that was famous for looking like it was moving, like a millions shadows were on it. It was crawling with butterflies. Billions of Monarch butterflies would stop there on their way to South America.

DB: I was disappointed in them because I'd imagined this vivid orange, but what it mostly looked like was fluttering bark. They reminded me of those lumpy rock creatures in *Flash Gordon* that would jump out of the rugged mountainside.

KK: I think I did pretty well with my first poem drawing. It was called "That Certain Something," from Kylie Minogue's French period, *Body Language*, with her imitating Jane Birkin and Serge Gainsbourg. I used bright Sharpies, the color of the Riviera. Yellow, green, purple. I didn't yet know how to draw anything, but I could underline. Years later I had a call from Barbara Gladstone, the eminent New York gallerist, who told me that one of her artists had seen this loser thing on eBay and admired something about it, and that he wanted to work with me. He wanted me to develop this style, the style of the fluttering bark. In the interim I had done a writing workshop for kids, and I wrote a poem called "A/Butterfly." The third line began with a C, and the fourth line began with a D. In Nabokov's story, "The Vane Sisters," butterflies are the spirits of the sisters who in real life were mediums. And now they become letters of words. They are spelling out the hidden meaning of the story.

When I got sick and couldn't write, I went through my drafts hoping to find one last thing I could write, and I had written out the beginning "A/Butterfly," and I drew a butterfly, pale blue like a tear. The rest of the page was blank.

Did you ever like butterflies, Dodie, when you were a little girl, maybe?

DB: All kids like butterflies, but I do remember one landing on my flesh and finding it unnerving. I feel bad for butterflies that come in contact with humans, the way they're captured and kids pull their wings off. I'm thinking of some song from our youth, "The Iron Butterfly of Love." Or am I getting that wrong?

KK: The Iron Butterfly was a band. You're thinking of "The Elusive Butterfly of Love."

DB: We listened to Iron Butterfly's "In-A-Gadda-Da-Vida" the first time we did acid, because we thought that would set us in the proper mood. I was fine with it, but my girlfriend practically started convulsing with panic.

KK: Because of the music?

DB: I don't know. She often had a hard time on the stuff, but that didn't keep her from doing it over and over. Do you ever have a compulsion to repeat something that scares you/tears you up?

KK: You know I do. Like whenever we have a fight, I want to make it up. It's scary to want somebody so much.

DB: You're trying to sweet talk me because I didn't want to write about drawing. I'm the worst drawer in the world.

KK: You're the reason they invented Photoshop so you too could become a famous artist.

DB: You mean, the reason they invented fabricators. When I first heard about fabricators I felt ripped off in life, thinking I would have gone to art school if I'd known you didn't have to be able to make anything yourself.

KK: That freed me, I'd say.

DB: I'm realizing more and more that the literary world has never been a good fit for me. I've always wanted to hang out with the artists.

KK: What magazines did we have growing up? It wasn't *Butterfly*, it was *Caterpillar*. How dreary! A caterpillar is a cement mixer or truck or something.

DB: Isn't it the thing from which butterflies grow? Like the prototype of a butterfly?

KK: In art you don't need talent, all you have to have is gesture. In writing you need talent; it's all about what they call craft.

DB: I would say gesture is the supreme talent. Everything else is craftsmanship. Craft taught in writing programs destroys talent. When we were at that purposely unnamed group reading last night, the one person who showed talent was the spoken-word guy, whose work was so rough and all over the place. There were hints of the real, for lack of a better term.

An example of gesture versus craft would be Lutz's "Playboys" series. She hired an illegal Russian immigrant to paint the Vargas drawings. She said Russians could do anything. They could make rubber cement out of old tennis shoes. There were supposed to be more paintings in the series, but the project came to a screeching halt when Lutz showed some of the paintings and, to her horror, the Russian went and saw how much they were going for. He got all haughty and asked for more money since he was the real artist. He couldn't understand that in this scenario he was merely a channel—a sort of trance-medium manifesting Lutz's vision. But I feel for him, the unjustness of class systems and labor.

Recently I found out that—after teaching two classes a semester at San Francisco State for nineteen years—all it would have taken for me to enter the pension plan was to have taught three classes for three semesters in a row. After that, it wouldn't matter how many classes I taught. Once you're admitted to the plan, you're in for good, and you can buy back the time you lost and get a full pension. In those nineteen years, the female poet who was chair most of the time, never offered me three classes, and now I'm having to fight for them. No matter how successful I become in life, in my heart I will always be Lutz's angry Russian.

KK: When Ugo told me—for it was Ugo Rondinone who had Barbara Gladstone call me—that he wanted me to draw pictures into my poems, I responded by saying I couldn't draw anything. He said—you can draw a smiley face, you can draw Hello Kitty, you can draw the rays of the sun, you can draw daisies and roses, and you can draw a butterfly. That's all you need.

DB: And, thinking of his clown show at the Berkeley Art Museum, you could also draw a rainbow. It was shocking how stunning it was, the room plastered with children's drawings of rainbows, floor to ceiling. It should have been totally cheesy, but it was marvelous, like jaw gaping.

KK: For me the '60s were Muhammad Ali, the greatest of all time: "Float like a butterfly, sting like a bee. The hands can't hit what the eyes can't see."

Week 5, May 26, 2019
Childhood Sex (Dodie)

DB: Our having gotten together and lasted so long was so unlikely, it makes me want to search for points of contact. Each of us grew up in the suburb of a large city—New York for you, Chicago for me. Both of us read incessantly as children (though that's true for most of the writers we know; it seems a recent phenomenon, non-readers wanting to become writers; I'm thinking of the many students in writing programs I've taught in who don't read books). We're both first-borns. We both have birthdays on holidays. And we both had sex as children.

KK: I should say that I wanted to have sex as a child, but I didn't often get to do it.

DB: But what about the Carey person you write about. Weren't you like 14 when you became involved with him? How old were you when you first had sex?

KK: I was 13 or 14 when I had sex for the first time. It took me longer than that to learn how to come, but I wanted to find sexual fulfillment with another person. That was the purpose of life. Or so we thought, our generation. I was 14 when I met Carey. I'd hitchhiked for a year before I landed him. I wanted someone approximately as old as my father, and almost as good looking, and I landed on him, who matched my ideal mate in many ways, and yet was also the exact opposite of what I wanted in a guy. I wanted somebody who was more like myself, my own age, my generation, with my interests, like a twin. I don't remember the first person I had sex with, but it was in the woods that surrounded my house. Probably neighbor boys, or boys from other parts of Smithtown, or strangers. I followed notes that were left in the trees, like leaves, promising sexual satisfaction. Later, I realized that since childhood my reading had programmed me to look for eternal love.

What year was it that you first had sex? Were you around the same age?

DB: It was 1962, and I was eleven, and unlike you, I wasn't looking for sex; in fact I didn't know what it was; I didn't know how babies were conceived. I got involved with a predatory girl my own age who was coming on to all the other girls at sleepovers. I'm the only one who did it; we pretended to be asleep. I guess even though I didn't know what sex was, I had a strong libido. The first time she stuck a finger in my vagina I came instantly, having no concept of what an orgasm was, but I remember thinking how all these things I'd been seeing in the world suddenly made sense, from Doris Day movies to bikini advertisements, to marriage. Everybody was flirting and preening to have this sensation, which felt good enough to drive you crazy.

And yes, I too was programmed to connect sex with eternal love. I stayed in that relationship for 15 years, though I'd say by the end of high school I was dying to get out of it. But I stayed. To compensate, I began a long history of cheating; that way I could be both inside a situation I was addicted to yet outside of it at the same time. Now that I'm older, I feel a lot of resentment towards her. I was too young to have sex, and being in a lesbian relationship with no support as a child, years before Stonewall, in Indiana, was hell. It added another layer of otherness to the otherness I felt profoundly, always having been somewhat of a misfit. On the other hand, if I didn't feel otherness I'd probably still be in Hammond, Indiana. So in a sense all that pain and alienation got me out of there, propelling me towards a richer life.

KK: Remember when we went to your twentieth high school reunion? You could tell who the gays and lesbians were because they looked so good. And the regular people all looked like their parents. One woman asked me if I was "part of the family," and I didn't know what she meant. She got out quick. When high school ended she moved to Chicago and designed interiors for McDonalds. All your other classmates were entering a contest about who had the oldest child. And who had come the furthest. And we had come from San Francisco, and people asked us how many children we had, and we just laughed, helplessly.

DB: And people kept saying to me, "Doris, you look so much better than you did in high school." Which was such a weird compliment, I didn't know how to take it in. It was a blast to sit at the queer table at the reunion and make fun of the other geeks who used to shun us.

KK: For some reason, everybody—and I mean like twenty people—at that gay table had all gone to Chicago, and all seemed to be intimate with the crime writer Sara Paretsky.

DB: From things you've both written and said, Carey treated you badly, and introduced some sex kinks, such as enemas, that make me cringe, imagining them done to a little boy. Do you have resentment toward him? You pose yourself as the predator, but do you also see him as predatory?

KK: I wasn't a little boy, exactly. I thought of myself as a young man with a desperate hunger for experience and wisdom. In the years that followed I saw more clearly how the system, how the multiple systems, propels itself forward by institutionalizing what you might call adult-child sex. I do blame the adults, sort of, and I'm glad that I went on to adult sexuality as soon as I did.

DB: What do you mean by "as soon as I did"?

KK: Before I knew it—let me illustrate—the number one song in the world the week I had sex for the first time was by the Beatles, a two-sided hit from 1966, both sides very experimental and strange. "Paperback Writer" on one side. "Rain" on the other. By the time I graduated from high school, it was David Bowie, Marc Bolan, and Lou Reed all the time. "You've got your mother in a whirl/ She don't know if you're a boy or a girl." "Rebel rebel, you've torn your dress/ Rebel rebel, your face is a mess." Experimental also, like the Beatles, but with the focus resolutely turned to deviant sexuality. And that's where I stayed until I met you.

DB: Are you saying I made you wholesome?

KK: Just the opposite. But what was that T-Rex song about a diamond star halo? "You're an untamed youth/ that's the truth/ With your cloak full of eagles/ You're dirty sweet and you're my girl." That's you, Dodie. I dedicated *Bedrooms Have Windows* to you, Dodie, in 1988: "Girl, I'm just a jeepster for your love." There were these machine world images of sexual desire: cars, motors, bombs, weapons, that promised hurt as well as salvation.

DB: I never listened to David Bowie until "Major Tom," but I was crazy about T-Rex and Marc Bolan. I remember he claimed he was going to change shape on stage, from one form to another. Unfortunately, I can't remember what the new form was supposed to be. He was a self-proclaimed mystic. But it was crazy back then, like my next door neighbor, Jeff, who did a lot of acid, believed his car could drive itself. I think that's because he often didn't remember the journey. One time we went to see Jethro Tull in Frankfort, Kentucky, and we missed the turn off and everybody was so stoned it took 2 hours for anybody to notice. There was a big flood and the concert was canceled anyway, and it was magical, driving through the ravaged landscape, horses standing in water, houses in water up to the second floor. No inkling of danger in the car, just this sense of time slowing down.

KK: We both lived with a lot of secrets: perhaps all young people do. Because we were writers we could give up our shame and our covert sexualities easier than others among our peers, our forebears, and those who have come after us. It's strange to think that we might have been the luckiest generation to have lived in the twentieth century. And all because of that one song, "Rain" by the Beatles.

DB: My girlfriend's and my favorite song to have sex to in college was Blind Faith's "Can't Find My Way Home." Beautiful, but kind of a sad song. We didn't know what we were doing.

I've never chosen to be with anybody for rational or wise reasons. And on the surface, you sounded like a horrible choice. An alcoholic homosexual who'd never had a mature relationship. But we could talk and I felt like I could tell you anything, and in many senses we saved one another's lives, and it was the best choice I ever made.

Week 6, June 1, 2019
Sylvia Plath (Kevin)

KK: How did you first hear about Sylvia Plath?

DB: I have no idea. I first got interested in her in the late '70s, when Janet, one of the first friends I made when I moved to San Francisco, gave me *Ariel* for my birthday. I wasn't expecting much, but I was blown away.

KK: In the late '70s she was already famous.

DB: She was famous as soon as she committed suicide. Successful before then, but not famous. Lately I've been astonished by how successful one can be in one's career, yet not hit that ineffable height of being famous. Being famous is like having a totally recognizable brand, like one's work becomes a logo.

KK: I think it's one of the things that bonded us because I loved Sylvia Plath too, and you stood up for her in a hostile climate. And yet, there were things about her that made me cringe, and you cringed at nothing. Your knowledge of Plath was much wider than mine. And you could actually quote passages from her, and if I tried, I would be grasping for straws, like "Daddy, daddy, you are so dumb." That can't be in one of her poems.

DB: No, a dumb daddy wouldn't have as much power.

KK: As an evil one? I first heard about her from that article in *Time* magazine that detailed her suicide and the attempts to put *Ariel* into print, and that must have been the '60s. My parents didn't get *Time* magazine but Professor Cassidy did, down the street, and there always was something in it about poetry. My god, I said to Catherine, my schoolmate in grade school, there's this guy called Frank O'Hara that got run over, not ten miles from here! And he's in *Time* magazine.

DB: Looking back, I'm amazed at how much, when we were kids, you could learn about poetry through the mass media. Like in *Time*—and I'm wondering why your parents didn't have a subscription, if it was too lowbrow or what. I talked my family into subscribing to the *Chicago Tribune*, just for their weekly book section, and there I learned about Neruda, for example. And I watched the 1966 series on the poets—Richard O. Moore's *USA: Poetry*—so I saw the Frank O'Hara episode, with its reenactment of him being hit by the dune buggy (or at least in my memory) and Anne Sexton playing lavish music to write her poems. All the incredible typewriters they sat at. I know I watched the whole series, but O'Hara and Sexton are who stuck.

KK: What broke the case for me was later in life when we got to meet Donald Allen and found out from him that, employed by

Time Life, was a fascinating woman called Rosalind Constable—hired by Henry Luce himself—exactly to put in these things and make people famous in the arts, often by death. The famous death of Jackson Pollock in a car crash—"death car girl" was driving the car and it crashed. All the famous things that happened in poetry were brainstorms of Rosalind Constable.

DB: What about somebody like Diane Wakoski—she, I imagine made herself famous, like she'd be one of those blogging/tweeting poets these days who develop a career from the ground up.

KK: Or like that one Instagram poet with the two four-letter names—Rupi Kaur. She's the most famous poet in the world. And she's 22.

DB: I never heard of her. I looked it up. She's 26.

KK: How can you tell if she has actual institutional backing or if she just does this through fellow fans?

DB: If she didn't start out with institutional backing, I'm sure she has it now. That's the way capitalism works, via absorption.

KK: Did capitalism/absorption work for Sylvia? What did she have that nobody else had?

DB: In many ways it worked against her. Plath is a genius, and she was turned into a cartoon. She worked incredibly hard to be successful and famous on her own terms—I'm thinking of her journals, where she rants about her jealousy of Adrienne Rich's success. But becoming a symbol of female rage and depression, that was so unfair. Male poets have been jumping off of bridges, forever, and they don't have to bear that burden.

KK: For me, I believe if she had never gone to England she never would have been famous. That it was just the moment.

DB: Hitching herself to Ted Hughes helped. She promoted him and boosted his career, and then she trailed along on his coattails.

KK: People must have been very jealous of her, the way that later on they got tired of Linda McCartney, another American heiress who came and captured another of their princes of poetry, Paul McCartney.

DB: Plath wasn't an heiress. She was middle-class, and after her father died of complications from diabetes, she was struggling middle class, raised by a single mother. Nothing glamorous about that. She had to create her own glamour. I never thought of people being jealous of her. Mostly you hear how selfish, moody, and bitchy she was. How dare she!

KK: And yet she rides on and on. No change in critical dictates have dethroned her, not entirely. At first people didn't like the way she threw Auschwitz around like it had happened to her, and her heaping of all the great tragedies of twentieth century history to make her heroines' domestic problems more intriguing, opening *The Bell Jar* the day the Rosenbergs were executed, for example. But she's still popular, and nobody remembers who the Rosenbergs were.

DB: I'd say that her point was that global trauma reverberates into our personal traumas. When the book opens, if I remember correctly, the heroine hasn't yet made her descent. The Rosenbergs were just setting the stage for how shitty America was at that point. Maybe we should write a novel and open it on the day Trump got elected.

KK: Or the day Freddie Gray got killed.

DB: We can all remember what we were doing when Kennedy got shot, or when the Twin Towers fell, so I like the idea of beginning something during a moment of shared trauma. All the divisiveness, and there are these moments where that falls away and the whole nation is suddenly tender together. Just a bleep.

KK: I remember when I first started teaching at CCA, it was maybe 2003, and yes, all of my students swore that nobody would ever forget what happened when the Twin Towers came down. Today, nobody knows and nobody really cares. I say, what do you all remember? And people like Andrew Durbin (under 30) remember the Sandy Hook killings, and they remember Hurricane Sandy, and that's it.

DB: I was teaching Writers on Writing when 9/11 happened, and my first reader was Daphne Gottlieb, and she stood in front of the class and said how, after that, her writing felt meaningless and she was ashamed to be reading it, and she started crying. It was intense, but in a good way. It's like she was speaking the subconscious of the room.

KK: What impresses people about Sylvia is that she moved heaven and earth to go and live in England, where she became so unhappy she killed herself—and that you can't escape your past. And maybe all of us feel this way in some degree or another. She couldn't escape Adrienne Rich; she couldn't escape the porch where she crawled under to die when she was an undergrad; she couldn't escape Otto and the bees; or Smith College and feeling like a freak, and perhaps knowing that one day Gwyneth Paltrow would play her in the movies, and Blythe Danner would be Aurelia, that even her son would kill himself.

DB: She also had an amazing life; when things were good between her and Hughes, it sounded like poetry heaven, fantastically generative and exciting. One way I've related to Plath is that she really wasn't a rebel; she was always trying to be the best at any shitty social value, from toxic femininity to formalist poetry—but she could never really fit in. There were these deeper parts of herself that subverted her dronedom, and when that broke through at the end of her life, her poetry was unstoppable, the energy and innovation. I've always been willing to conform, but the part of me that can see what bullshit that is, rebels every time. Thank god, or I'd have lived the most boring life, and I'd have stayed in relationships that would have destroyed my writing. Again, the suffering, for me, has been the biggest gift. I've sometimes felt that situations were against me, but more often than not, I can see how I was manipulating things so I'd be ousted from places that were toxic to me but which I couldn't get myself to leave. Do you relate to this pattern at all? You seem much less conformative from the get go.

KK: I do believe that Plath outsmarted herself by having those children and swallowing that Kool-Aid, and there she might well have known that that would lead to her death. Also, England was on the cusp of glamor in 1963, when she died, but it was a hideous place for everybody but a very wealthy few.

DB: And it was the worst winter ever and she was really sick and worried about money—and having to take care of these kids.

KK: And Assia calling her on the phone in that little Persian voice, saying your man he belong to me now.

DB: Your version is a bit twisted, but what about my question above, do you personally relate to that pattern?

KK: I've almost gone to places which would have wrecked me, utterly, but some sense of preservation steered me away.

DB: Like what, for example?

KK: The thing I'm thinking of now is the subject of my new monograph. That is, how in the early days of AIDS, when none of us knew what a mammoth tragedy it would become, I stopped myself several times from making the kind of flip joke about AIDS that I later crucified Tom Clark and Ed Dorn for making. I was furious with them because it was so close. It might have been me who had given out to lesser poets the AIDS Award for Poetic Idiocy. This haunts me. Plath was only 30 when she died. She had the typical lifespan an AIDS patient would have had twenty years later. That's haunting too.

Week 7, June 8, 2019
Now (Dodie)
Bruce Boone and ICU nurse visiting

DB: Kevin, what do you want to say to the world?

KK: I honestly thought that chemotherapy was not going to be a big deal. I thought I was going to have 4 or 5 sessions without any difficulty. Instead after one session I wind up in a place where I don't know where I am, in grievous pain the likes of which I had never known—both mental and physical contusions.

BB: Kevin you've always been so polite; you can't just say fuck you.

DB: Actually, since Kevin got sick he's said fuck you to many people. He's learned to be bitchy and not take any shit.

KK: In Redwood City they tried to move me to another room, a shared room—and I said to them, I am Kevin Killian, what you're doing is garbage.

DB: And it worked. Kevin got a fabulous private room where I could spend the night. You once said to me that you felt like if you'd be able to speak up for yourself more, you wouldn't have gotten sick.

KK: Yes, it's true. As I've come to view my life in the poetry world, I realize that the struggles of poetry led me into a hideous depression that wound up giving me cancer.

DB: But what about all the love in your world. You know you're a very loved person.

KK: I thought that the very poets who gave me cancer were the ones who loved me most.

DB: You're talking about a very small population, and one of your main pain-in-the-asses, you were never close to. What about all the others who didn't hurt you?

KK: The Bard of Avon said it best, "They who have the power to hurt and do none, etc."

DB: Bruce, you've been around warring and disappointing poets since the '70s, how have you come to terms with that?

BB: At some point a few decades ago I decided the poetry world was all fake and stopped.

DB: Kevin, what about all your artist friends?

KK: I love them because they bring in money.

BB: You set a high barrier.

DB: Let's get off the poetry scene.

KK: I'm at Kaiser in room 3212 and it's a dud. Not one good thing has happened here. Twelve hours of my hopes being washed away like soap bubbles barreling over a viscous basin. There's one work of art that intrigues me. It looks like a crucifix made of raw steel in some Spanish friar's chamber.

DB: What is that?

RN: It's a sling for lifting patients.

DB: What I've learned from all we've been through is how insanely generous the people we know are.

KK: Yes. I guess I'm feeling bitter.

**Doctors arrive to insert Kevin's breathing tube.
June 11, 2019**

DB: I was going to write this in my journal, but my fountain pen has come apart and is all gunked up. Usually I can get it started again, but not tonight, which I took as a sign to write here instead. Hard to figure out what to do with this project, which you were so invested in and which we had so little time to work on. Before they put you on the breathing tube, you said, "We had a good long time together," and yes we did, but not nearly enough. You could still come back for a bit and I would love that more than anything, but nobody seems hopeful of that.

After dinner I returned to the hospital so I could spend some time alone with you. You looked peaceful, but when I held your hand I couldn't feel your presence, like I have before. I held your left hand and thigh on and on, but felt nothing, and I thought that perhaps you weren't as present as before, that you were leaving, and I told you that was alright, that you should do what you needed to do. I thought how your presence wasn't connected to your body, and I felt an assurance that that presence wouldn't leave me.

And then I felt a pulsing in your hand and thigh, and my hands began pulsing in synch with your pulsing, and I felt calm and my heart opened. It wasn't my love, but your love, which entered my heart. I said goodbye to you and drove home in a state of grace, my heart radiating love—your love in my core, radiating out from me.

Saturday night, when they put in the breathing tube and David Buuck and I spent the night at the hospital, I was exhausted, and I was able to get the night nurse to help me set up the one chair in the visitor's lounge that pulled out into a bed. You would have loved the nurse. She had tattoos down her arms and was very performancy, dramatically announcing her every move in your room, as she changed and adjusted your medications. David and I fantasized she was a former exotic dancer.

As I lay in bed, I tried to imagine healing yellow light surrounding you, and failed miserably. I was trying to force something that just wasn't there. Then I remembered the butterflies we wrote about here, and I saw a swarm of butterflies flickering around you, comforting you and sucking all the alien material out of your chest. And I could feel the butterflies doing the same for me, and I felt an intense connection between us, regardless of distance. I thought to myself—he may come out of this or he may not, and either is okay. I knew you were okay, and I felt at peace.

Since then as I've held your hand, I've spoken to you about the butterflies, told you they were fluttering in your chest, healing and comforting. And I could feel your energy relax.

Dr. Strako called this morning. I guess she's been visiting you at the hospital the past couple of days. I asked her if she believed it helped to sit with you, and she said it definitely did help. She said on some level you knew I was there, and even if I sat and read a book, it helped, just my being there. She said you and I were among the special 10% of her patients, meaning we were together for a long time and still loved each other—people who could be together for 50 years and still want to have breakfast together.

I know you sent me this love tonight, you sparked my heart so I wouldn't feel afraid. I will miss you so much, but I know you'll never leave me.

June 13, 2019

DB: Even though your immune system collapsed today, they reduced your sedation. When Ariana Reines and Julian Brolaski visited, you smiled, despite the god awful breathing tube, opening your eyes wide as if to allow all the good will in the world to beam out at them. I said, "Would you like Ariana to sing you a song," and you nodded yes. Ariana sang Peter, Paul, and Mary's "Autumn to May," with backup by Julian.

AR: Oh once I had a downey swan, she was so very frail
     She sat upon an oyster shell and hatched me out a snail
     The snail had changed into a bird, the bird to butterfly
     And he who tells a bigger tale would have to tell a lie.

DB: Tender butterfly, teller of tall tales, I love you.

15

Anniversary

Monday, June 15, is the anniversary of the death of writer Kevin Killian, who was my husband for 33 years. The thought of spending it alone during this shelter in place is both terrifying and numbing. I have discovered an enormous capacity for numbness, which continues to surprise me. Before Kevin's death, I couldn't bear to think about the horrors of widowhood. Joan Didion's *Year of Magical Thinking* seemed like the most dangerous book in the world; I wouldn't touch it. After he died, I read it compulsively.

For all other anniversaries this past year, I went to Los Angeles. The first trip was the weekend of July 3rd, our wedding anniversary. I stayed with Matias Viegener. His partner was out of town, so he gave me their king-sized bed. I hadn't had a full night's sleep since the beginning of June, but that giant bed swallowed me; I spent most of the weekend in it, gloriously unconscious. "Here, let me do this for *the bereaved*," Matias said as he fixed me a snack. "I love saying that word—*the bereaved!*" Most people acted like they were afraid of me, but here was Matias, calling me *the bereaved* over and over again, in an exaggerated, goofy manner and I found myself laughing.

My memory of those early days is spastic, but if I squint and strain my mind, I see a group of us at Taix, an old school French restaurant in Silver Lake. I know this dinner happened, and I'm pretty sure it was for our anniversary. Who was there. Hedi El Kholti, my editor at Semiotext(e). Hedi's partner, Colm Tóibín. Writer and editor Andrew Durbin who was living in New York at the time. Matias must have been there. I think I ordered risotto. Andrew and Colm talked passionately about James Baldwin, and afterwards I ordered a collection of Baldwin's essays. We were supposed to raise a glass of wine for Kevin, but I don't know if we did.

Kevin's birthday was Christmas Eve, so I again stayed with Matias. I went to two holiday potlucks and one sit down dinner. On the fourth night there I went to a Thai restaurant with Bradford Nordeen, and now it's coming back to me that on the first trip, for the 4th of July Bradford took me to Echo Park, where we looked at ducks and lily pads, and afterwards I posted pictures with happy captions on Facebook. Yes, things are great here in Los Angeles two weeks after the death of my husband, why wouldn't they be. Even though Joan Didion taught me that doing well should not be a goal of my widowhood, I was embarrassed by my incompetence at keeping it all together. I still am. Another memory: after Echo Park, Kaucyila Brooke held a tiny barbecue for me. "Don't expect me to perform mourning for you," I said when she greeted me, and she smiled. Flash of a picnic bench in Kaucyila's backyard, Sheree Rose is sitting across from me reminiscing about the death of Bob Flanagan. Kaucyila's big floppy long-haired dog seems to be everywhere at once.

For my birthday, February 14, I spent the first two nights at Hedi's and the second two at Matias's. Having both been born on holidays, Kevin and I understood that sense of feeling special but also of feeling eclipsed on Our Day. When Kevin (who would get over 500 birthday wishes each year on Facebook) died, I again felt eclipsed by the outpouring of social media mourning. For me his death was intensely private, yet it dominated the poetry/indie publishing/art Facebook and Twitter feeds for a week. His death was bigger than David Bowie's. There were tributes published by those who loved Kevin and whom he loved dearly, by those he politely suffered, and by assholes who don't have a right to speak his name, but who speak anyway.

This piece is not a tribute; it is about his loss, his terrible loss. Little of Kevin is here. Widowhood is an anti-space. There is the world. There is you. The connections are erratic and confusing. Hedi's former partner, who died of cancer, was a politician, so he understood that feeling of having the privacy of his mourning violated by all these others who claimed a piece of Bill. On my birthday weekend we sat at Hedi's kitchen table until three in the morning, drinking wine and talking about our beloveds' deaths. I'm surprised by how similar Bill and Kevin were; no one ever reminds me of Kevin.

Kevin is lauded for being this easygoing guy, always there to support and entertain, someone who could brush off the pettiness and drama that the rest of us in writing and art scenes suffer under. In truth, Kevin was an extremely sensitive person who couldn't deal with conflict. He would do anything to erase conflict. For instance, Kevin's role as a biographer and editor of the poet Jack Spicer lead to occasional vicious attacks in print due to some perceived error in Kevin's scholarship or interpretation; things so minor that in the real world they'd be laughable. The way Kevin would handle that is to befriend his attacker through flattery and kindness, whatever it took. He could convert sworn enemies into allies. Kevin loved musicals. His core sense of sanity was so fragile he needed to believe the world was as beautiful and glorious as a musical. When we were getting involved, back in the early 1980s, one of the first things we did together was watch his video cassette of *West Side Story.*

Tributes to Kevin go on and on about his kindness. In the *Laurel Canyon* documentary, which I watched last week online, fame is portrayed as this force that doesn't so much corrupt as it destroys. But Kevin reveled in his big fish in a small pond type fame. "I am Kevin Killian," he would proudly say, as if the world should sit up and take notice, and he'd flash a big smile as if it were a blessing. His kindness was authentic—he was truly a good person—but his kindness was also a shield. He needed to be loved, not just by me, but by everybody, and if somebody didn't love him, the musical couldn't play and he was devastated. I couldn't protect him when he was alive, and the longer he's dead the less I try. One thing I learned from Matias, who is Kathy Acker's executor, is that all attention is good attention. Like Kevin, I need to say yes to everybody.

16

Jeffree

Here's the backstory. The writer Kevin Killian, to whom I was married for 33 years, died last June. People say I'm handling it really well. People are wrong. It is all-absorbing living in a state of afterwards. Rationality eludes me. I have become a creature of impulse and instinct, ravenous for media images that resonate with my unendurable. Even though I own a TV with a couch in front of it to sprawl on, I mostly watch stuff on my tragically aging iMac. I watch these hours of TV series, movies, and YouTube videos with an uncriticality which reminds me of the 1990s when I obsessively wrote about horror films. From Kathy Acker I learned to turn off the censor and to embrace the screen with a childlike awe. Back then it was a sort of discipline. But now it's spontaneous.

I cried while watching *The Morning Show*; I cried at the Nick Cave concert when he ended with T-Rex's "Cosmic Dancer." "I danced myself into the tomb." I cried during the *Wild Wild Country* documentary, and *Schitt's Creek*, and *Broad City*. Every show I watch seems to be about friendship, family, community, coupledom—those who have or find these treasure, or those losers outside the system who are going crazy. There were others—*Marriage Story*, *House of Pleasures*, *Fleabag*, *Alfie* (1966 version),

The Returned, Spaced, The Crown—I cannot remember what I've watched—*Call My Agent, Gameface, Late Night, Miss Americana*—I cried through all of them, even that drecky Ricky Gervais *After Life* series. And of course I cry when self-made makeup mogul Jeffree Star's 9-year-old Pomeranian, Diamond Star, dies. And when he breaks up with Nate, his boyfriend of five years. As he sits up in bed before a pink flocked headboard flanked with cupids and vines, wearing what looks like velvet pajamas, surrounded by his four Pomeranians, Jeffree's voice trembles. "I can't believe he's not here right now." "My soulmate is no longer with me." He ends the video with, "There just needs to be more love." And every cell in my body resonates a big YES.

When Jeffree collaborates on a makeup palette with his best friend Shane Dawson, I weep like a fool. A bottom line in Shane's multi-part series chronicling their partnership is that Shane is poor. Despite his tony house in a gated community, in this story, Shane is poor. "I have less money than people think I do," he says by way of explanation. I accept this because it is necessary for the narrative arc, which is that Jeffree is making poor Shane into a millionaire because of friendship, because of his love for Shane. Business meetings are punctuated by Shane sneaking off to the bathroom, squatting down and crying out of fear and gratitude. Lots of YouTubers cry, but fans comment that Shane's tears are real.

We the viewers extend Shane and Jeffree's love by buying their costumey makeup. The morning their Conspiracy Palette launched, fans bought with such a frenzy, they broke the internet. Shane presents us with a wonderful montage of excited people opening their palettes, magical boxes of glowing colors, oohing and aahing—overcome like they're having an ecstatic vision. Getting a palette is taking home a snippet of a saga they watched six episodes of, a relic. I write in my diary, "This is as good as capitalism gets." I can't help but order the Mini Controversy Palette—even though I have such sensitive skin I only wear nontoxic makeup—and these atomic colors, you can tell just by looking at them, are far from that.

Successful YouTubers furnish their homes with huge complicated couches with chaise lounges built in where guests cuddle beneath fuzzy blankets before lit fireplaces. They have vast outdoor patios and pools. Fame forces them to live in hermetically sealed environments, but still their lives revolve around community, friendship, family. Though Jeffree is infamous for dramatic public fights and the trail of bodies he has left behind, the new Jeffree has learned how to love because of his relationship with Nate. To underscore his intimacy with the viewer, Jeffree often films wearing only a robe or a towel.

There is nothing wrong with corporate sponsorship to fund the dream. While my lefty friends are out resisting late capitalism, YouTube influencers have adapted to it and are thriving, like arthropods that survive a nuclear attack. In their Gucci slides and designer jogging suits, they relentlessly copy the Kardashians. To create drama on their shopping sprees to Target or Home Depot, they exclaim, "Oh my god, I am so scared right now." Jeffree fills his mansion with pinball machines and an armed vault loaded with Hermes Birkin bags. He's abandoned the "Barbie pink" of his old home for a more sophisticated black and gold palette. He pushes the cliché of nouveau riche into a new dimension of unapologetic tackiness. YouTube presents a version of personality on steroids, and Jeffree is a master of this, making it seem natural. He's like an acrobat of personality, leaping effortlessly out of the screen and into our lives.

Like the Kardashians, YouTubers love fast food. Jeffree and his staff excitedly eat McDonalds as they fly cross country on a private jet. YouTubers have a particular obsession with Taco Bell, which they rave over, even though the ones I watch all live around Los Angeles, where amazing authentic Mexican food thrives. A taco truck on Sunset Boulevard is going to knock Taco Bell—with its wormy curls of white and yellow cheese—out of the ballpark. In his final video with Nate, in which Jeffree shows off their gaudy new ten-bedroom mansion, he stands beside its massive marble dining room table and says, "I can't wait to eat Taco Bell on this." I snort out loud and think to myself, this guy is a genius.

The last time I had Taco Bell was last spring in Redwood City, a nothing place south of San Francisco, on the outskirts of Silicon Valley. Kevin was in the Neurosurgery ward at a hospital there, and I slept most nights in his room on an easy chair that pulled out into a cot-bed. We tried to pretend we were on a fun vacation together. Across the street was a Taco Bell, and thus the unmelted plasticky cheese strewn across its tacos I associate with hospital disinfectants.

Kevin too loved junk food and designer clothing. At an opening artist Mario Garcia Torres was wearing a pair of shiny turquoise Paul Smith shoes. When Kevin asked him about the shoes, Mario said he just bought them, that they were on sale at the San Francisco boutique, and Kevin rushed over and bought a pair. And after that, all his shoes were Paul Smith purchased on sale. In his poem "Who" he critiques his own constructedness: "always the quaint uppermost in mind,/ my mad strive for personality."

Jeffree's relationship with Nate reminds me of my marriage to Kevin. Jeffree, who denies being trans, is radically genderqueer.

Nate is not gay. He's just a straight guy who's into Jeffree. One could argue that I'm bisexual, but Kevin never claimed that label. He was a gay guy who through some miracle fell in love with me. When Jeffree puts on women's clothes it's not like he's doing drag, or suggesting a female gender. He's doing glamorous. He pushes what it means to be "male" to the breaking point. What's going on with him is beyond current categories, harkening back to a time before gayness was invented, when dick-hungry men met in bars named after a color and a bird, the Blue Parrot, the Golden Pheasant. Jeffree has done what all we freaks long to do—triumphed *through*, not despite of his otherness. He's every beat up young fag's dreams come true.

First thing every morning I check out Jeffree's latest story on Instagram, a dailiness that mirrors relationship. His posts are often banal, at times boring, but in the morning he's always there. Jeffree looks up at the sky and says, "Hi Sunrise! How ya doin', Sis?" And I join his Pomeranians dashing across the tiled courtyard, squatting and pissing before the dramatic Hidden Hills vista. All of our names begin with D—Drama, Diva, Delicious, Da Vinci, Dodie. Jeffree points out his long thin shadow. "People say my shadow looks like Slender Man." He laughs. "Am I? Am I Slender Cunt?"

Bee Reaved

after Christina Ramberg

Bee Reaved reads online that *Alem*, the root of the Hebrew word for widow (*almanah*), means "unable to speak." The Modern Widows Club website extrapolates: *Isn't that the way you feel? Like someone hit the mute button. Or, you are unable to articulate how you feel or what you are really thinking. Or, is anyone even listening to your cries at all?* She wonders if the writer is a fan of Rilke: *Who, if I cried out, would hear me among the Angelic Orders?* Who, indeed. She finds herself returning to her journal with the passion she felt for it in high school, exuberantly inking the unshareable. In typography *a widow is a last word or short last line of a paragraph falling at the top of a page or column and considered undesirable.* Its Old English form *widewe* derives from an Indo-European root meaning "be empty." Bee thinks back to a line she read in a Jungian book in the 1980's, about women whose lives fall apart: *the contained has lost its container.* It is the container that is empty; not she.

Her untouched body coalesces into a semblance of a female form; some parts are out of alignment, leaving gaps. There used to be two but now there is only one. Bee knows deep down she was always one—but now she is a super one, a heavy molecule, and all the things the other one used to do are left up to her—

hauling the recycling down the stairs—she's hopeful she's going to have enough money to survive because the other one left things behind—clothing books manuscripts access to an undefined amount of funds. When she removed the bills from his wallet she felt like she was robbing him. Now she has things she always wanted—an office of her own, enough closet space. She mocks up excitement for her newfound expanses, then clenches with guilt, then she doesn't give a damn. She'd live in a heap of garbage to get back her other one.

Memorials for him colonize social media for a week, more than a week. Online voices wail and wail and wail and wail as if there were no end to their mourning. She calls up Matias in Los Angeles and says, "It feels like the world is consuming him and there will be nothing left of him for me." Matias says the world is small but the other one is huge. There will be plenty left for her. She quips, "You're becoming quite the guru." Bee cancels her reading in Norway. She doesn't have the energy. Her writing lies there, flat as the page it's written on. She buys new sheets, switches the ink in her fountain pen from blue to black, compulsively reads the Twitter feed of a writer she believes is a fraud. The fraudulent tweeter calls Bee's other one "a saint."

Always there is a gap between the image you think you're tossing out to the world, and the image the world receives. Thus the cruelty and brilliance of Diane Arbus, who wedged her camera into the heart of that gap. Click. Bee feels awkward as a giant standing beside her parents in a working-class doilied mid-century living room, bending her head to avoid the ceiling. Her home looks like a cyclone hit, and the vacuum cleaner is broken and there's nobody but her to replace it. She throws on some clothes and somehow makes it to the car, but when she starts the engine she notices a horrible stench. She turns off the engine and gets out of the car. The bottom of her deeply-tracked hiking shoe is covered with shit, human shit. She rubs her sole in some standing water and then on the edge of a curb, then more water, then in some leaves, then more curb, but the pattern of her sole is too deep, too ornate. She gets back in the car and drives to Bed and Bath Beyond, reeking of shit. She enters the store and heads straight to the restroom, where she finds beside the toilet a scrub brush. She takes off her shoe and holds it over the toilet and dips the brush in the water and scrubs and flushes the shitty toilet water and scrubs and flushes and scrubs and on and on, it takes forever, the grooves are so deep, so impacted. Finally the shoe looks clean enough. Bee wipes residual shit from the toilet seat and flushes one last time. Then she looks at her legs—fuck—her black knit pants are spackled. She walks to the sink and wipes down her legs with damp paper towels, reminded of the tragically unwashed who ride city buses, other passengers covering their noses and moving away. Her efforts are inadequate and her legs smell like shit. When a store employees enters, she feels caught and hurries out the door, trailing funk through bright, polished aisles. No one to save her, no one to call and hyperbolize this into a sick joke.

Bee dreams about a person—a man—who is confused and a bit frantic. He says, "I've changed so much, will they recognize me when they see me? It's been six weeks." She wakes up, knowing it was her other one. As she gets up to pee, she says out loud, "I'll recognize you."

With a thick black marker, on the side of the van belonging to Walter Skold, the man who discovered Jack Spicer's grave, her other one wrote a passage from Spicer's poem "The Holy Grail." *The grail is the opposite of poetry. Fills us up instead of using us as a cup the dead drink from.* Like much of Spicer's poetry, this is a mindbender for Bee. She ponders it for a few days and concludes she is neither filled nor a cup. She is the contents of the cup. The dead are sipping her through a straw. She complains to Matias that the internet turned the death of her other one into a circus. "But," Matias replies, "he loved circuses."

In the Intensive Care Unit machines drive the patient, his breathing, heart rate and blood pressure. Programs are adjusted, electricity zapped to the chest, catheters inserted in penis and anus. Slow and thick, time hovers like smog. Doctors and nurses don't give you hope, but they don't take it away either. They say you never know in the ICU, things go up and down in the ICU. Despite their meticulous interventions, the patient's condition permutates relentlessly towards death—not a natural death—a death Bee had to ask for. "Pull out the tube and let him die." The medical staff assured her this was a rational decision, but there is nothing about it that isn't fucked. When his sedation was reduced, her other one opened his eyes and rolled them upwards, and then he spread his arms wide and raised them. He looked like a beatific saint having a vision. Remembering this, the welling in Bee's chest races to her mouth and she clenches down a scream; enduring the unendurable, moment after moment, like an endless drip of water that erodes stone.

His ashes arrive in the mail. Two black women stand outside her front gate, the older woman holding a corrugated white plastic mail bin, with the package inside, as if she dare not touch the box. She has an expression of enormous compassion, and says it makes her sad to deliver this. Bee scrawls her name on a digital device the younger woman hands her, and picks up the box of ashes. It's much heavier than she'd imagined. Carrying that irreducibly heavy thing up three flights of stairs, with each flight its weight becoming more leaden, Bee starts weeping silently—

though inside her a hysterical widow shrieks, her black mourning dress flapping as she throws herself on her husband's grave, clawing the earth. Bee places the box of ashes, unopened, on the floor of the living room closet. From the door latch she hangs an arching sprig of indigenous motherwort picked from a friend's garden. The six weeks between her other one's diagnosis and his death were a gift. High from steroids and feeling superhuman, she was beautiful to him, their apartment was beautiful, the bouquets of flowers crowding every surface were beautiful, as were the ribbons and papers that wrapped them when they were delivered. After his one visit to the oncologist, they found a little lunch spot called Just For You where they ate eggs and cornbread and beamed love at one another like newlyweds.

When he was dying she said to him she knew he would always be here with her in spirit, that they would always be together, and then she felt his presence expand beyond his stiff gasping body, filling her. But now that he's gone she no longer senses him. It's as if he's dissolved into the masses of social media admirers, abandoning her. Only once has she heard him in her head, saying "Bee" in his distinct East-coast inflected voice. A psychic tells her, "He's gone, but he's looking down at you." If he loved her he wouldn't have left. He'd materialize in the steam from her tea kettle, would rattle the pots at night, levitate his ashes, shock her with cold spots. If he loved her, she'd be swooning right now in his icy embrace.

She stands at the edge of the page and leaps off.

Why were there two postal workers? The older woman did all the talking and seemed to be in charge, so perhaps the younger woman was a trainee. Or perhaps the uncanniness of such a parcel rendered it too precious for a single employee. The older woman wore white plastic gloves and did not touch the package, which was labeled CREMATED REMAINS. The box is on the living room closet floor. Bee does not want to look at it. She signed for it then picked up the untouchable thing. It was heavier than she'd imagined.

Bee goes to an art museum. In the lobby she stumbles upon an acquaintance, and says, "Hi." Light and casual. The acquaintance cocks her head, contorts her face into an exaggerated frown that begs Bee to perform widowhood, and exclaims, "I am so, so sorry!" Bee says, "I don't want to talk about it," and heads for the galleries. Mostly headless, the female torsos on the wall are both abstracted and material, collages of textures that fibrillate fore and ground, their surfaces totally flat, as if they were pressed beneath glass slides, squishing affect. Bodies in uneasy tension between form and splatter. When Bee held her other one while he died, there was no transition. Click. His features turned angular like landscape in the John Ford Westerns he so admired. Monument Valley. "Did you see that?" she said to her sister-in-law. "He's gone." *The human body is not a thing; it is a procedure.* A few feet away, a docent goes on and on about the art, punctuating her memorized drone with anecdotes meant to amuse. Bee's other half could have done a better job. She stares blankly at the paintings. *Flatness. Fragmentation. Shattered feminoids put back together in new order, cool as a mummy's tits.* His knowledge of contemporary art seemed boundless—looking at art with him was like having her own remarkable docent—and it strikes her how she's lost this envelope of knowledge. *Petrified organs, mostly recognizable by gesture.* That's what he was like, a loving envelope, and henceforth she'd have to find things out for herself, which sounds so exhausting that suddenly she can't bear to look at art without him *chilly stillness without end* and she rushes from the museum. A widow's version of the Stendahl

Syndrome. *Everything spoke so vividly to her soul. Ah, if she could only forget. She had palpitations of the heart, what in Berlin they call "nerves." Life was drained from her. She walked with the fear of falling.*

Whenever Bee attends a literary or art event, she is accosted by condolencers with droopy sad puppy faces. They look cartoony and monstrous as if wearing masks by Paul McCarthy. The dog faces bounce up and down, saying, "I am sorry." Their hands reach out and touch her. One novelist clamped onto her arms, stuck his face in hers and exclaimed, "This is terrible! You must feel terrible! How terrible!" People say he behaved this way because he's Irish. It's as if she were a child or a pet whose body belongs not to herself but to whomever wanted to fondle it.

On the bus ride home, Bee thinks of the art school lover she had in her twenties, who repeatedly told her she was "too much," how he photographed his former girlfriend bare breasted on her back, covered with a sheet of glass that pressed her large breasts flat as fried eggs. She looked like a specimen beneath a giant's microscope. And then her mind hops to that photo of Sarah Lucas sitting in a chair all butch in distressed jeans and spread legs, with gooey-yolked fried eggs on top of her breasts, managing to be obscene and cartoony all at once. Joe Ferriso, who made a watercolor portrait of her and the other one just a couple of weeks before he died, said he and his wife were naming their unborn daughter Violet for he and his wife were a mix of red and blue. A wonderful reductiveness, like a late Eva Hess or a Sarah Lucas sculpture: fill a sack with something bulbous and that equals tits. Bee longs to embrace an aesthetics of condensation, to write a scene with stick figures fucking, paring down the rigmarole to its barest form. She prefers the intricacy of a slab or a slice to the blah blah blah of the whole. At her mammogram, the technician smashed her breast in a vice and flashed it with radiation, converting it to a ghostly profile. The nipple disappeared and the breast looked like an image from space, the topography of a dead planet, or the moon, rough fissured surface against a flat black. To represent dense breasts the meme-maker places cantaloupes inside bra cups.

For the next three months, Bee has a 66% increased chance of mortality over what she had before her other one died. She dare not tell anybody how when the mourning crashes down on her and panic sets in, this 66% gives great comfort. Online she reads that a widow's goal is to move from distress (negative stress) to eustress (positive stress), as she sets the trajectory for her new life. She must restrain, re-form, compress, and bind her lumpiness into a clean smooth line.

He was a frightened child and Bee was a slightly more capacitated child bumbling about with him. Adults would have gotten a second opinion, adults would have dumped the oncologist who was so doom and gloom they called him "Dr. Death," the oncologist who plowed ahead with chemo when anyone who knew what they were doing would have seen her other one was too weak for it. When she yelled at the oncologist on the phone, he said the other one apparently wasn't as healthy as he acted—as if he'd tricked the doctor into giving him the drugs that killed him.

Bee dreams about her other one twice in one morning. She's in the kitchen, having just checked in on him as he lay in bed, something she frequently does, to make sure he's okay, make sure he's still alive. Then she remembers he isn't here anymore, and the checking in must be a memory. Then he appears in the kitchen, supine, floating in midair at the same height he'd be in the bed, and she shouts at him, her face bulging with passion, "I can't do this!" She wakes to total silence. His silence. Her silence.

A silence that feels endless. The other dream was more vague—a flash of him standing, looking at her, confused and perhaps frightened. Of course she takes notes. Her broken parts are sticky—not assertive as glue, but tacky like a bad moisturizer the skin never quite absorbs—repellant to touch, gathering dust. She can tell she's kind of numinous. People gape at her like an exhibit in a science museum—her body a series of slices, one half-inch thick, preserved in plexiglass or a cow with a window cut in her abdomen, revealing her marvelous digestive system. Bee is bearing what they all fear. She imagines digital eyes absorbing her, then judging and expelling her. The same internet that stole her other one, will steal her, and there will be no place to hide.

In 1822 a Canadian fur trapper suffered a massive gunshot wound to his stomach, leaving a hole in his abdomen that could not be sewn shut. Stomach acid disinfected the wound from the inside out, and even though he had this gaping hole, the trapper lived to be 83. His doctor peered into the stomach window and learned the secrets of human digestion. The doctor noticed that when the trapper was sick his digestion slowed, establishing an important link between digestive processes and disease. Shock too shuts down digestion, as Bee experienced firsthand after her other one died. Inspired by reports of the trapper, Russian physiologist Ivan Pavlov carved windows into the stomach of dogs and discovered that classical conditioning could prompt dogs to salivate on cue. A modern window on a cow's side is shaped like a porthole and called a fistula. The current fistulated cow housed at Cornell University's veterinary college is named Blossom. Before her there was Stella, and before that Elsa. Online Bee finds a photo of a guy in a turquoise T-shirt with his arm stuck through the fistula of a black and white cow, reaching into her stomach. His arm is encased in a giant plastic condom. The title of the photo is "How to Fist a Fistulated Cow." The guy reaches in and pulls out a handful of half-assimilated grass. The storm inside the cow's body is not reflected in her placid exterior.

Bee sits in the cafe at the Twitter Building, eating too much, downloading every phone message the other one left her; she does it compulsively like a pained little rodent. Dozens of messages. She "shares" each one by tediously emailing it to herself. She imagines creating an audio collage of every time he says "I love you"—not passionately, but hurried and casual, often no more than as a substitute for good bye—because that's what 33 years of marriage is, a study in redundancy and variation, and so much love there is no need to fixate on any particular moment of it. The audio collage is a great idea, she thinks, sometime in the future, when she can steal herself to listen to his messages, when the sound of his digitized voice wouldn't destroy her.

Plague Widow

Driving to the Castro, Bee Reaved feels hyper emotional, as she often does in the car, Nick Cave's *Ghosteen* on repeat, and she thinks—this is what it's like to live without hope. Six months after Kevin's death, friends left her to fare for herself. Other widows warned her this would happen, that everybody would disappear before she was ready. One widow she no longer talks to said, "Wait and see, you're going to have a total breakdown." Now, with the terrible isolation of lockdown, Kevin feels even more dead, a thudding suck-all-the-light-out-of-the-room dead. Reality is crumbling for everybody, and no one believes the old world is ever going to return. Instead of providing comfort, the ghoul in the White House feeds off of chaos, inciting it wherever he can—more homeless more starving more corpses conspiracy corruption, racial antagonism through the roof. It's no surprise protests erupt into riots. Rip it all the fuck down. Bee hates vicious righteousness. A stupid tweet by a nobody, meant as a parody, somehow goes viral and the internet offers up death threats. Canned Mexican beans, you are over. Racist woman walking your dog without a leash, you are over. On *The Daily Show*, host Noah Trevor jokes that the only thing not to have been canceled is the coronavirus. Since Bee herself was once canceled, she is mesmerized by public shaming. She spends hours piecing together the full story—how things have been taken out of context, twisted, lied about. The searing unfairness arouses within her a twinge of stalker love for the accused. Bee cries in her car but longs to scream, to shout out something vile, to spin her head around like a possessed Linda Blair.

The cat leaves a lumpy brown puddle on the bedroom floor, enters the living room and shits on the rug beside the bags of clean laundry that Bee digs through for things to wear rather than putting the clothes away. The cat then shits in the threshold between living room and kitchen, and finishes with a flurry in the middle of the kitchen floor. Luckily, Bee doesn't step in any of it. That evening, as Bee is slipping into bed, exhausted, the cat looks at her and leaps off, spraying urine mid-air across the bed. Bee cleans it up, googles cat euthanasia, and texts her misery to Donna. Donna suggests she cover the bed with a waterproof camping tarp, and she sends Bee an Amazon link.

Dream: Kevin is excited about helping Bee sort out her life. He says he will take on this big pain-in-the ass project of hers—a project she can't imagine him capable of handling. He's right there, so real, she could reach out and touch him. Then she's alone with a phone to her ear. He's still excitedly talking through the receiver, but now she remembers he's dead, and she thinks— he can't do anything to help me.

Bee gets up in the morning and the camping tarp has slid down the bed, onto the floor. She steps barefoot on the crumpled heap. It's sopping wet—cat urine. She bundles up the tarp, carries it to the bathroom and throws it in the clawfoot tub. She plugs the drain, runs cold water, squirts in some lingerie wash, and swishes the tarp. She turns off the faucet, leaves the tarp to soak, and starts her coffee. That afternoon as she walks toward the living room window, she steps in a pile of cat shit. She wipes the remaining shit off the floor with a tissue, sprays the spot with lavender and mint scented pet stain remover, scrubs it with a paper towel, sprays it again with Zero Odor, which Donna recommended. Then she flushes the tissue down the toilet and tosses the paper towel in the kitchen trash. She remembers the tarp. She empties the bathtub, shakes as much water off as she can, retrieves two lengths of rope—white with red speckles—steps onto the back porch, which is three stories up and windy. Bee drapes the tarp over the railing. She threads the ropes through the grommets in each corner of the tarp and ties it to the railing. Stepping back into her home office she notices a stench and finds shit encrusted on the bottom of her clog. She takes the clog to the clawfoot tub, runs hot water over the sole and scrubs it with a grout brush, sprays it with "natural multi-surface cleaner," scrubs and rinses until all the grooves in the sole are clear, then she sprays the sole and the brush with lemongrass citrus disinfectant. She puts her clog back on and washes her hands the COVID-recommended twenty seconds, singing "Happy Birthday" twice, to mark the time. When she gets to "happy birthday, dear—," she always sings the cat's name. They've been together for fifteen years.

As she sits at her desk writing this piece, she can hear the tarp flapping in the wind. She imagines the sail of an ancient boat—like in a poem by Robert Bly—and her life moving forward over choppy waters towards something or other. She hates Robert Bly. Sexist asshole. If she could cancel anybody, it would be Robert Bly. The next morning her downstairs neighbor complains that water from the tarp dripped down to her porch, and Bee loses it.

Dream: She says something unkind to Kevin and there are tears in his eyes. When she wakes she can't quit obsessing about the thousands of unkind things she said to him over the thirty-seven years she knew him. In her living room, boxes are stacked precariously up to shoulder height, filled with books and archival material. They're heavy and she can't generate the energy to haul them three flights down to the basement. Because of COVID, no one will come over to help her. The clutter makes it difficult when she smells cat shit, to find it. No one will come over. She spends her days talking to a screen. It's like living in Future World, except instead of sexy spandex space suit she's wearing yoga pants with a frayed crotch and a sweatshirt. The Zoom psychic tells her the energy in her left leg isn't running freely because she's holding a lot of Kevin's energy there. The psychic says Kevin's full name out loud then begins to clear out his energy. Afterwards she says that as soon as she said his name, Kevin appeared and she said to him—you've left your energy in Bee's left leg, and he said—yeah, I know.

Bee gets up to pee. The bathroom waste basket is spilling over with empty toilet paper rolls. Flash to childhood, putting a tube to her mouth and going "Rooty toot toot." Walking back to the bedroom she steps barefoot in a small bit of shit, hobbles back to the bathroom, scrubs her foot with a disinfectant wipe, cleans up the splat that remains on the kitchen floor, washes her hands. Then she slathers luxury sanitizer on her hands and feet. The scent of rose geranium and rosemary is divine.

Somewhere there's shit, somewhere close, but Bee can't find it. She turns on the flashlight on her iPhone, lies on the floor and looks under the bed. Nothing, but then she sees it, a foot from her head, a huge splash of diarrhea all over the bramble of cords plugged into the surge suppressor next to the nightstand. It takes her fifteen minutes of patient wiping and spritzing to clean it up, all the while fearing electrocution. There are still shit specks wedged in the crevices of the textured USB cables. There's shit and piss all over the place, it's useless. Bee is barely able to manage a shower, to organize, take her clothes to the wash and fold, feed herself, get anything done. She found herself bragging to Donna that she changes her underpants every day. She feels old and irrelevant as the characters in the final episodes of the French TV series *A French Village* (2009–17). For five seasons their town was occupied by Nazis. Life as they knew it was over. They were doing their best, and then comes the liberation and they're condemned as collaborators. They walk through a France they no longer recognize, wearing really bad old people makeup. That's how aging feels to Bee—like she's a young person trapped beneath sagging prosthetics. TV assures her that dying never means the end. Through the pornography of flashbacks, Marcel is no longer executed by a German firing squad; Marie is no longer lynched in the town square, her body left hanging in the tree as a warning to other mouthy women. When they were alive, Bee would huff at how irritating Marcel and Marie could be, but when they return from the dead, her love for them is unstoppable. It's been over a year and Kevin's ashes remain on the floor of the living room closet, in the package they arrived in, unopened.

When the cat shits on the kitchen table, next to her food dish, Bee googles cat dementia. The symptoms are all there. Before Bee started giving her CBD, the cat's anxiety was through the roof. She was turning feral, pacing around the kitchen emitting wails that started at a low tone then slid to a full-throated high pitch, extremely loud—like nothing that ever came out of the cat before. It was horrible. A cat psychic said that because of her colon cancer, the cat was stuck in her lower chakras, in survival mode. The psychic said the cat was freaking out over her body's betrayal. The resonances with Kevin's personality changes at the end are too poignant. No matter how many times Bee googles "frontal lobe tumor," she'll never know what was stress and what was metastasis. Kevin died too soon. She was supposed to care for him, but he died too soon. Two months later the cat got sick. When the cat dies there will be no one left to care for, and Bee fears her humanity will shrivel like an unwatered plant.

Bingeing on 72 episodes of *A French Village*, Bee expected all the French she took in college to suddenly kick in and she'd understand what the villagers and Nazis were saying, but it didn't happen until the court case. The lawyers with their over-enunciation sounded like the recordings she listened to ad nauseum in Language Lab. The violence and humiliation those occupied endured—their resistance, their living off of soup and chestnut puree, their grief and passionate sex with the wrong people—all that remained subtitled gibberish, but the lawyers' denatured bureaucratic French anybody could understand. She washes her face the YouTube-aesthetician-recommended sixty seconds, singing the Alphabet song twice, to mark the time. They've recently changed the rhythm of the Alphabet song. Instead of "elemenopee," it's now "L. M. N. O. P.," each letter enunciated as distinctly as a French lawyer. One guy complained, "They changed the ABC song to clarify the LMNOP part, and it is life ruining," and his tweet was liked 105,000 times.

Sometimes when she's shoving cancer pills down her throat, the cat will pee on Bee's leg. The cat has weaponized her cute little body. The cat shits under her desk, and almost daily in a doorway, where Bee is most likely to step in it. The cat's placements are beginning to feel purposeful, ritualistic. Like a Pennsylvania Dutch hex sign. The cat misses the doggy pee pad and sprays urine across the bottom dresser drawer. As she's typing this, cat shit fumes assault Bee. She is reminded of the 1950s movie gimmick, Smell-O-Vision, in which odors paired to what was happening on the screen were released into the theater using a system of tubes called a "smell brain." Bee sets aside her laptop and hunts for the mess. The cat is leaking everywhere. The more Bee tries to hold it all together, the more life feels like a reverse-motion cartoon where the painting unpaints itself. Jewel-toned spray bottles improve her morale, purple for stain remover, hot pink for odor eliminator.

She and Kevin laugh and play and argue, it's wonderful. Then as always, reality slips in and she's bummed with him for pretending to not be dead, for deceiving her. When she wakes up, the cat's trying to squeeze in beside her. Bee turns over and says, "Come here you little pisspot." Pisspot—where did that come from? Her mother called her that when she was a small child. "You little pisspot." A working class endearment. Another pang of loss arises. Bee imagines a long series of memories sputtering behind her—dead memories, their hyper-saturated color fading to black and white then flipping to negatives, their decaying emulsion misting into air. *Each of us deserves to be forgiven, if only for our persistence in keeping our small boat afloat when so many have gone down in the storm*—Robert Bly.

Bee walks from room to room, eyes fixed on the floor. Nothing. Then she checks her office. Underneath her desk is a box of beans—from her bean club—that has been sitting there for several months. Across a cellophane bag of green lentils, she spies a blotch of runny shit. She picks up as much as she can with a tissue, wipes off the green lentils with a paper towel and throws the lentils in the trash. She wipes off a smaller blob on the edge of the Rio Zapes, opens the other end of the bag and empties the beans into a bowl. The other bags seem to have had minimal contact. She searches for 5 empty quart Mason jars, finds three clean ones, one dirty, and she empties out another containing musty flaked coconut. She washes the two jars, dries them with a towel, blasts them with her hairdryer. Then she transfers the rest of the beans into jars. Yellow Eyes. Black Caviar Lentils. Wild Rice. Vaqueros. She thinks of Psyche, separating the lentils from the beans and grains. One of many tasks she performs after sputtering the lamp oil on Eros' thigh. There's more cat shit on the sisal rug, more shit packed into one of the complicated wheels of her Herman Miller chair. Bee fetches a scrub brush and a bowl of warm water. The more she wipes, the deeper the shit burrows into the sisal fibers. Bee can't remember what happens to Psyche when her tasks are completed. She gets something that she is now worthy of, but what is that?

After their first week in lockdown, her friends were already feeling bored and lonely and (even though they didn't admit it to her) afraid. They were texting her day and night, and the flakiest among them was urgent to make a Facetime date. When it comes to aloneness, they're such amateurs. Whereas Bee is a pro. Widows are the prima donnas of aloneness. She wants to tell these masked babies—don't worry about it being more than you can endure—because if that happens you'll go into shock—and when you're hit with unendurable loss, shock is the most wonderful gift. Reality/your feelings/memory/the horror of your situation are on the other side of this long narrow tunnel. You couldn't reach them if you tried. All that muck is replaced by calm. Behind your stumbling words and confusion and even your tears, there is calm. And erasure. She wrote in her journal those early days—"that Kevin ever existed is harder to grasp than his loss." With everyone alone, the aloneness of her mourning is violated. She's the one who's supposed to be wearing the widow's weeds, the special one who's set apart, who receives and banishes visitors, capricious as a queen. The plague is stealing her thunder. It's as if Bee's grief has seeped out and filled the world. Her isolation is now the human condition. She watches the end of the world, wizened, hunched over, doing whatever it takes—foraging mushrooms and berries, squeezing sustenance out of a mere strip of bark. She places the empty toilet paper tube of American culture over her mouth and chants, "Rooty toot toot."

For everything Bee wrote since the early '80s up until the week he died, Kevin was the first reader. He was perfect—adoring, but ruthlessly honest. It wasn't always easy. Once when his changes went on and on and on, she shouted, "If you think my writing is so fucked up, next I'll just give you my notes, and you can write it yourself." Sometimes she was softer, interrupting him with: "I need a compliment." As she writes now, it's like he's still there, his brain racing with ideas. She finds herself reworking passages with edits he would have made. Derek McCormack told her that after his horrific experiences with cancer, the way he wrote beforehand no longer made sense. He had to figure out a new way of writing. Bee thinks about this at least once a day. Is the same true for her? If she started writing in a manner Kevin wouldn't recognize, would she lose her last connection with him? Derek underwent an arduous surgery in which hot chemo was sloshed throughout his abdomen. Bee googled the procedure. Its slang term is "shake and bake," "shake" for the swishing and "bake" for the heat of the chemo. The cruelty of the epithet shocks Bee. This is the humor of someone who has seen too much, too often, someone who is struggling to maintain their humanity. All that pent-up terror and rage, it either explodes inside you or is ejected in a burst of uproarious spittle. To laugh at chaos is to fuck chaos.

Bee walks into the living room and says, "Why am I here?" She's talking out loud to no one, and her aloneness slaps her. This sort of aloneness destroys people, yet most of the time she hardly registers it. This is not living, she thinks. This is afterlife. The cat squats in the doorway and lets out a runny shit. When Bee finishes wiping it up, since she's already on her hands and knees, she does a few cat-cow stretches. Her body is so aroused it's unendurable but she feels no desire, not even a smidgen, so she ignores it. The body won't stop. I'm here, it shrieks, I need need need need love need touch need some fucking attention. The body is unrelenting. She lets it go for another day or two, then slides a vibrator up and down its clit until she finds a spot inflamed and tense as a zit that's ready to burst. When she comes, the cat—who's been sleeping at the foot of the bed—is suddenly beside her, all purrs, rubbing herself against Bee's arm. Bee laughs and says, "Get away from me, you perv." Vibrators give the worst orgasm—beneath the rumbling of the buzzy machine, quakes of tender flesh barely register. Kevin was so good with his fingers, she called him a virtuoso, playing her body like a violin. Long, flat and bendable, the vibrator looks like the lovechild of a tongue depressor and a stretched out wad of Silly Putty. It's mint green with ten speeds and patterns. She washes it in the kitchen sink then takes a photo of it in the dish drainer to text to Donna.

Since the vibrator pic was such a hit with Donna, the following week Bee texts her a photo of the urine-soaked asphalt beside her car from when she went for a walk in the Castro. Because of COVID, there are no toilets anywhere. When she returned to her car she had to pee so bad that right there, right in the busy residential neighborhood, she sat sideways in the driver's seat, half in/half out of the car, pulled down her pants and pissed on the street. Donna replies that her urine photo is "the most superb text I have ever received in my entire life." She particularly enjoys "the rogue drops of urine ON THE FOOTBOARD OF THE CAR!!!! Completely, utterly sublime. Bravo, madam. Bra-fucking-vo!"

Just as Bee is about to fall asleep she smells something. She gets up and follows the scent, but she can't find anything. She turns on the flashlight of her iPhone, gets on her hands and knees, and looks under the bed. A pile of diarrhea. Even if she lies on the floor on her stomach she cannot reach it, so she frantically scans her brain for something, anything that can be repurposed as a long-handled scooper. By the time she's cleaned it up (sort of) she's so wound up, sleep is hopeless. She retrieves her laptop, logs into Hulu, and continues watching Season 5, Episode 12 of *A French Village*. Villeneuve has just been liberated and chaos reigns. A mob of townspeople accuse Hortense of being a Kraut whore. They spit on her, strike her, chase her barefoot through the street, haul her in a cart to the town square, where a chair appears for Hortense to sit in as rustic men hack away at her blazing red hair with scissors. It's a carnival, everybody laughing and hooting and craning their necks for a better view, children included. Hortense sits tense and unmoving, bottling her terror inside. She wasn't a whore; she was in love with her Nazi—the top Nazi in charge of the town's occupation. In the midst of grim bureaucracy, they staged a grand, problematic love affair much more exciting than those of the repressed Party-first Communists. The fury of the townspeople is fueled by their jealousy over all the beautiful clothes, booze, and gourmet food lavished upon Hortense, when most of them were starving. The Nazi was charismatic and refined. He and Hortense were thrillingly vivid together. Great onscreen chemistry, Kevin would have said. Even after the Nazi tortured Hortense—he was never portrayed as a nice guy—Bee found herself longing for them to be together. The series often made Bee cringe at her own desires. Nothing is simple and everything is impure. The hair clipping is finally done. Hortense's ragged bald head accentuates the gaunt angularity of her cheekbones. The camera peers in even closer, filling the screen with bloodshot eyes ringed with clumpy smeared mascara, rivulets of tears flowing downward. Medieval French proverb: "Dogs keep on pissing, and women keep on weeping."

During the liberation of France, 20,000 women were accused of collaborating (aka sleeping) with the German invaders. Like Hortense, they were publicly humiliated. Some were kicked to death in the streets. Bee first learned of these women from the song "Shaved Women," (1979) by British anarcho-punk band Crass. The lyrics to "Shaved Women" are minimal and repetitive, mostly "shaved women collaborators" and "screaming babies." On the back of the record's cover is a photograph of a shaved woman who is surrounded by a jeering mob as she walks through Chartres holding her German baby. Just when it seems obvious that the time frame of the song is the 1940s, the lyrics dip into a more modern era: "Shaved women shooting dope/ Shaved women disco dancing." Women who shave their bodies in order to conform to a hetero-normative dating aesthetic, is that too a form of collaboration? When Eve Libertine belts out "screaming babies," she enunciates "screaming" at a normal register and "BABIES" as a shriek—screaming BABIES screaming BABIES screaming BABIES over and over, the words grow silly and frantic, a hysterical chant that fuses horror and comedy. The lyrics online read: "babies screaming" rather than "screaming babies." If the online lyrics are correct, in Libertine's rendition there is a weird pause between babies and screaming, an unnatural syncopation reflecting a world order that is out of whack. When Libertine shouts "shaved women collaborators," it's not clear if she is critiquing the torture of these women or if she's assuming the position of someone in the crowd announcing their arrival, their shame. The song dips into multiple positions at once—and all of them are shattered. "Shaved Women" doesn't need the extended melodrama of A French Village to create (anti)meaning. The song throws us into the heart of an irreducible frenzy that hails everything and nothing.

Bee was too shy and anal for the San Francisco punk scene, but she envied the women. They got to be nasty—nasty as men, nasty as children. The daughter of a construction worker, Bee was raised to be nasty. Ribald, over-sexed, and under-classed, she came across as a Baby Boomer Wife of Bath. Employers and local literati alike recoiled from her. Her writing mentors, who were Marxists, told her that writing was a middle class occupation. "If you want to be a writer," they said, "you need to learn to be more middle class." Thirty-three years married to Kevin, fighting over his critiques of her public performance, she learned to behave herself. Mostly. When you stick a dog in a tutu a ballerina you do not make. A nasty woman never stops being nasty. She just ceases to bother.

> I nil envye no virginitee;
> Lat hem be breed of pured whete-seed,
> And lat us wyves hoten barly-breed;
> And yet with barly-breed, Mark telle can,
> Our lord Iesu refresshed many a man.

Instead of going to sleep, Bee sits up in bed with her phone and googles "Wife of Bath feces." While the Wife of Bath makes more references to urine than any other pilgrim, she never mentions shit. In "The Wife of Bath's Urinary Imagination," Shawn Normandin of Sungkyunkwan University, South Korea, posits that Chaucer wrote her that way because back then "antifeminist traditions often represented females as liquid, dripping creatures."

Listening to "Screaming Babies" on repeat, Bee imagines a reverse-engineered version of herself, a vulgar girl who no longer is ashamed, a girl whose words go BOOM BOOM BOOM their thuds so dense they decimate those who would straightjacket her. Bee has the leak of widowhood upon her. She goes forth impenetrable, one of those hard-edged women who having lost everything important to her, can now shuffle through adversity unfazed, like those old ladies in her childhood neighborhood, widows who fled the persecutions of WWII—"DPs" her father called them—the kind of widow who when her toilet is clogged, rolls up a sleeve of her housedress, plunges her arm in the bowl and roots out the impaction with her hand, an aproned widow who acts like she'll kill you if you step on her lawn. A widow doesn't care if she's alone, doesn't care if she's fat and old and undesirable, doesn't even care if she dies. The cat stops in the doorway and makes a sloppy balloon-popping sound. Crouching with her ass puffed out like a blowfish, her front legs extended, she releases an explosion of diarrhea then walks away. Bee's senses are assaulted, over and over and over. Brute repetition replaces an entire system of meaning. That doesn't stop Bee from reading messages in all of this. The cat is saying *I'm an animal, I will not be personified, will not be contained by your bourgeois expectations, will no longer pretend that the institution of pet is not a form of slavery.* That night Kevin comes to her. It's one of those untranslatable dreams that instantly erase themselves. Bee cries out, struggling to stay inside the dream, his loss a leaden wedge spreading over everything. The alarm rings and she gets up and walks towards the back of the apartment. In the living room there is a main dump then a patch of smaller satellite dumps across the room. In kitchen a scattering of smooth brown drops are arranged like the petals of a flower masterfully stitched on a linen cloth. She just misses stepping in them. The solidity of the cat's shitting pissing puking body keeps Bee from floating away. In the morning as she feeds her, groggy and irritable, the cat cries desperately. The cat throws herself in front of Bee's feet as she walks to a cabinet to fetch a can of Mack and Jack. The cat has no sense of past or future, no logic, no patience. A ball of rumbling Id. The cat makes the slightest squeaky meow and Bee knows to turn the kitchen chair in the optimal position for her to jump on the chair then onto the table. As Bee strokes her with a soft boar bristle brush, the cat purrs wildly. She says, "I love you, my little poopy poo."

19

Chase Scene

April 4, 2021
Dear Kevin,

Suddenly, two angels in dazzling white clothes appeared. The women were terrified, but the angels said to them, "Why do you look for the living among the dead? He is not here; He has risen!" I didn't plan to finish this letter on Easter. The timing just happens to align with the deadline Hedi gave me. I've been writing to you since Thanksgiving. I was planning a quick, tossed off thing, inspired by a letter Hedi is writing to his deceased partner, Bill. Hedi's directness, his tone of unmediated vulnerability, excites me. Hedi says the only reason he can go there is that it's been four years since Bill died. But your death is still in its infancy. I've not yet moved into that sentimental remembrance phase. My time with you is tucked away like the box of your ashes that sits on the floor of the living room closet. I never open that door if I can avoid it. But once I started this letter, I couldn't stop writing. There's no attempt to present things in the order I wrote them. As you know, I've always been more of a gut chronology type of girl. I looked up how the date of Easter is determined. It's the first Sunday after the first full moon after the Spring Equinox. I knew it was a pagan hybrid, but Easter is witchier than I imagined.

Side note about the "I": Dodie's gone. I don't know where she is or when and if she'll be back. Imagine she's a star on *Grey's Anatomy* and blind items are popping up on those gossip sites you read every morning, about difficult contract negotiations. For now it's just me and you. Bee Reaved and Kevin. I have access to her memories and desires, and a prototype of her personality. I'm not sure you'd even notice the switch, but these days folks are all about transparency and accountability. I'm going to proceed using a simple non-meta first person. Back in the '80s when we got together, people had the energy to get all arty, but not now. When I say "I," think Bee with an aura of Dodie. Or vice versa. It doesn't matter.

Writing to you is all-consuming, I don't have the bandwidth for anything—or anybody—else. I ask myself: you're living the life of a desert monk (a metaphor I stole from the internet) so why aren't you lonely? Myself answers: because the nonliving are the best listeners. You always had a beneficent ear—one of the reasons I fell in love with you. In the beyond that ear has grown vast, too vast for petty human insecurities. No longer do I need to worry about your feelings for in your vastness you know that everything I do is love. Even if I told you to fuck off, your beneficent ear would hear me loving you.

I bought you a niche at Cypress Lawn, two rows down from the communal niche Jack Spicer rests in. Funded by Kickstarter donations. Kim, the sales rep, couldn't understand why I'd want to put you there. Despite the gorgeous skylights, that part of the columbarium is no longer fashionable. People like the newer wing, with its tacky glass-fronted niches, where they can arrange dioramas of photos and objects of significance around the departed's urn. It's been so long since anyone's been entombed in Spicer's wing that the person who made the metal faceplates retired, and no professional could be found to replace him. So Chris Bell is fabricating a faceplate. While we were working on this, Chris installed a permanent piece for the Exploratorium. There are all these concrete columns in the bay near Pier 17, and atop them Chris installed clusters of tiny mirrors mounted on steel rods that extend for nearly 100 feet. Screwing all those rods into mirrors was arduous. The installation is called *Sun Swarm* because it's all about reflecting light. And now he's applying his incredible precision to your niche, examining a nearby niche to see how it's constructed. Surprisingly the groundskeeper opened one that had a urn in it, as if jostling the dead was no biggie. Chris built a frame and cut a sheet of copper to exactly match the curved top edges of your niche. I have a photo of him with the top half of his body inside the two foot by two foot concrete chamber, as he traces an arc. It's both banal and eerie. The niche was supposed to be a surprise, but it's taking forever with civilization as we know it collapsing, etc., but I want you to know you won't be on the closet floor forever. Your brother-in-law Dave went above Kim's head and talked to the owners. What a great human interest story, he told them—the biographer of the poet Jack Spicer, a poet himself, is buried next to his subject matter. Newspapers are sure to pick up on it, resulting in lots of free advertising for Cypress Lawn. Dave finagled a 20% discount—the biggest one they've ever given. Vets only get 10%.

Cypress Lawn would never allow it, but I wish Chris could encrust your faceplate with mirrors that would reflect the stained glass skylights, an effervescence of greens and reds. In an article called "Splendor in the Glass," which I include since it's punning on your favorite movie by your favorite star—Natalie Wood—I discover that the ceiling glass wasn't by Tiffany after all. It was designed by Harry Ryle Hopps of San Francisco's United Glass Company. Architect Bernard Cahill wanted ceilings that allowed in natural light because he believed "that the antidote to the darkness of death should be an abundance of light and color." The glass in the earliest catacombs, where you'll be, was imported before WWI from England and Germany. Eventually Harry Ryle Hopps—a name you would say sounds like a serial killer's—moved to Los Angeles and worked as art director on *The Thief of Bagdad*, which I just watched the beginning to—the stylized yet ornate grandeur of the sets, the animality of Douglas Fairbanks' acting—I'm using every ounce of discipline not to write about it here.

A month after you died, Sylvia was diagnosed with virulent intestinal cancer, and so that's been the focus of my mourning, cleaning up cat shit. You wouldn't have been able to deal with it. Sylvia did remarkably well for 13 months, followed by a month of rapid decline. One Wednesday evening around 6 pm, I was standing at the kitchen sink and a bolt of energy—it was like a fist—slammed me in the chest—I gasped and thought—Sylvia's died. I found her behind the couch on her side, legs outstretched, a small pool of fluid drying around her mouth. Rebeca Bollinger came over to help, and I joked—dead husband in the closet, dead cat behind the couch. Rebeca brought a cardboard box and a towel for Sylvia's body, and we drove her to the late night emergency vet on 18th and Alabama. Karen—the chiropractor Karen—told me how she had ordered an impression of her cat's pawprint—it seemed to mean a lot to her—so I ordered one for Sylvia. It came in the mail a few weeks later, and like your ashes, I never opened it.

Each night when I finish working on this letter, I watch *Grey's Anatomy* and cry. I don't cry for you. I cry for characters, for their touching moments, for their losses—of life, of love. Juana recommended the show. I wonder if she too cries. Last night they killed one of the main doctors, George, and since you taught me that when that happens there's always a backstory, I googled it and you were so right. Donna had told me that one of the stars was fired for making a homophobic slur. It was Isaiah Washington. Allegedly he called T.R. Knight, the actor who plays George, a faggot. Because of the scandal, Knight wanted to come out as gay, but Shonda Rhimes (as you know, the show's creator) was against that, so his part was cut way down. For the first nine episodes of Season 5 he only appeared on screen for 48 minutes total. Knight quit, and the show gave George a horrible death, so disfigured that the other characters don't recognize him. When they realize that John Doe is in fact George, that was a great crying moment.

In a dream I am instructed to give Donna a pseudonym more fitting for Bee Reaved's sidekick: Pea Culiar.

Night after night on *Grey's Anatomy* I return to the hospital—to trauma, MRIs, breathing tubes, and unexpected tragic outcomes. As I said to Pea Culiar, it's like being home. In a recent episode they left in the breathing tube when they zipped up the body bag. Would they really do that? I keep thinking of the body bag they zipped you into, it floats on the periphery, a black blobby cloud of almost memory. I can't imagine I actually saw it, not with the way Kaiser controlled access to procedures. On the show, the family often stays in the room when the patient crashes and the Code Blue team is shocking them back to life, or attempting to. At Kaiser some nurse would have whooshed me out of the room like a dust bunny. Maybe the nurse mentioned the body bag when she was telling me I needed to arrange for someone to pick you up. After you died, I went out to lunch with Maureen and Nancy, then at home, all alone, I somehow managed to call a crematorium. Bob Glück gave me a list of places, based on their Yelp reviews. I chose Tulip because of its stupid name. And its 5-star rating. The whole thing cost around $600. I see why so many fringy arty types get cremated.

The world has turned upside down. Imagine a sci fi movie where there's a global pandemic. Even though hundreds of thousands of people have died in the US, many do not believe COVID-19 exists—or they believe it's caused by 5G cellular networks. People wear masks on the streets, and some of these masks have a small, thin flexible metal strip where the mask hits the bridge of your nose, so you can adjust it for a custom fit. The metal strip is an antenna for 5G, which proves that wearing a mask will kill you—people who believe this have been elected to Congress. I'm always impressed by the comprehensiveness of conspiracy theories and cults. The attention to detail is stunning. Seven months after you died, there was a rigorous lockdown—then more flexible lockdowns. My classes are all online. Except for Rebeca, Glen, and Linda and Erik (one time each), no one's entered our apartment for a year. This aloneness is vast. I'll find myself slipping into an emotional hypothermia, and just when it starts to feel dangerous, Pea or Bradford will text, or Hedi will call—one time Apsara showed up at our front gate with a bouquet of flowers—and my heart thaws. All that love you lavished upon me those thirty-some years, perhaps I still have a store of it to draw upon, and that's why I can survive on so very little. I don't know. Everybody is going at least a little crazy. It feels like a quasi death, or a confused realm between death and life. You wouldn't like it. You'd spend most of your time online lighting up everyone's lives. Day to day it would waver which one I would resent more: you hogging the computer or you ignoring me. You always needed constant stimulation. Before the internet you read a grocery bag full of books a week, mostly foraged from thrift stores and the public library.

After your diagnosis we continued to make plans, to prove we believed there was a future for you, that you would be alive six months or one year down the line—and in that spirit you bought us tickets for Nick Cave at the SF Symphony. Mid-October, 2019, four months after you died. I went with David Buuck instead. Katy Bohinc went to his concert in New York. She texted me a video. It's a more intimate venue. Katy sweeps to the stage and hands Nick Cave her most recent collection of poems, with a hug. He says, "Thank you. What do you want to know?" Katy replies, "My dear friend, poet Kevin Killian passed away earlier this summer, and he loved Kylie Minogue, and you did a thing with her, and I thought, that if Kevin's listening somewhere out there, that maybe he would like to hear you talk about her a little bit." So Cave talked about how wonderful Kylie was, in your honor.

Thanksgiving, 2003—you were stuck in the hospital because the doctors at San Francisco Kaiser couldn't decide on stents or open heart surgery. The worst of it was your unplanned withdrawal from cigarettes. The nurses gave you a pass on your heart attack diet, and Marcus and I got turkey dinners to go from Home, where Maggie Zurawski waited tables. Though I barely knew Maggie, she said somebody needs to take care of the caretaker, and she came over and washed my dishes. A foreshadowing of the astonishing kindness with which people treated me after you died. Except for the Antagonist, of course. He was a dick to both of us before you died and he continues to be. I want to tell the world, this is the person whose treatment of Kevin was so torturous, Kevin blamed him for giving him cancer. If you're capable of haunting anybody, of throwing them into a state of pants-shitting panic, put the Antagonist at the top of your list. And, yes, I'm aware that you would tell me to cut the stuff about the Antagonist, that it makes me sound petty. So be it. Towards those who hurt you, I am remorseless as the winged goddess Nemesis, scales in one hand, sword brandishing in the other. My feral working class us-against-the-world devotion drove you crazy. You would have preferred me to have been written by Noel Coward. Off-color, but sophisticated.

The antagonist introduces disorder, thus the antagonist is always death.

On the phone Hedi and I were talking about which films we were streaming. I told him how with you there wasn't much room to negotiate what we watched. It was either what you wanted or you acted distracted and bored, so I gave up, and for years hadn't seen anything that wasn't big budget. You to me: "I like to see the dollars up there on the screen." Me to Hedi: "At least I never have to watch another fucking car chase again." Hedi told me to check out *To Live and Die in LA*, that it had a great chase scene. He said the cars drive the wrong way on the freeway, which is everybody's worse nightmare. Not my worst nightmare, but I don't live in LA. And so I watched it, and what an amazing movie. I jumped right into a hyper-focused research spiral. I read about the history of chase scenes/innovative milestones in the genre/what makes an effective chase/old-school live-action versus CGI. I watched a documentary on William Friedkin—and this awful film he made after his career had tanked, showing a real life exorcism. On the internet some killjoys found an early recording Friedkin posted of the possessed woman, and audio specialists compared it to the woman's voice in the movie, and determined that Friedkin had enhanced the movie voice to make it sound more creepy. Like you, Friedkin couldn't control his storyteller impulses. Maybe in real life the woman did sound more demonic than what the film captured. Maybe an approximation of the real was more real that the real—exactly the point of Tim O'Brien's use of fictitious material in "How to Tell a True War Story." An ancient memory comes forward—San Francisco, the late '70s, when I was making corporate slideshows, and the owner of the company, an ancient New Yorker named Gus (he was probably 50) who used to work in advertising said that in the old days to photograph tomato soup they would put marbles in the soup to make it look bubbling, but because of truth in advertising government regulations you couldn't do that anymore. Gus felt this was a great loss to bubbly soup photography. In a chase scene the antagonist and the protagonist often get confused, and the audience doesn't know who to root for—the good guy or the good driver.

The chase, according to Friedkin, is "the purest form of cinema, something that can't be done in any other medium, not in literature nor on a stage nor on a painter's canvas." The chase shows the obstacles, shows how bold or brave or desperate or even stupid the characters are to escape or pursue, shows how far they are willing to take it. There's build up, shock, and aftermath. There is tension and fear. There is rhythm and flow. Cars zoom like jets. The cars' relationship to one another is a form of geography. The audience is the passenger. It is rare to walk down the street with a machine gun—but everybody's been in a car, everyone's felt what it's like to lose control. Moviegoers sit on the edge of their seats, their feet on an imaginary pedal, ready to slam on the brakes.

When our Yaris started to erratically race and lurch forward, I figured there must be a problem with the transmission or something, but since it only happened when you drove, I was pokey about making an appointment with a mechanic. Things came to a head when you sideswiped a parked car, without realizing it. You noticed something, but it was windy out, so you thought it was the wind. A good Samaritan busybody took down your license and left a note for the car's owner. The insurance said that this was hit and run—a felony—so we were worried for weeks a cop would appear at our front door and take you away. But no cop ever came and no charges were filed, and the insurance paid, and I don't even think our rates went up. You decided not to drive after that—except to take me to my endoscopy. As soon as you started the engine it was obvious you didn't have control of the pedals. Traffic was heavy, and I was terrified as the car jerked forward then slammed to decelerate. Several times you almost rear-ended the car ahead. On the way home I was wobbly-headed from the anesthesia, so I didn't give a shit. After that I had to drive you everywhere, which you found humiliating, but I tried to make it seem like an adventure.

When he was forty, Spicer collapsed without ID and ended up a John Doe at San Francisco General. It took days for his people to find him. He died, and it took another forty years for the caretaker of his memory—you—to discover where he's buried. You took poet after poet—local or visiting—there. I only went once. Spicer's niche is too high to reach, so you wheeled a ladder in front of it, and poets would climb up and read his poems to him. There was also a round of bibliomancy, using Spicer's *Collected Books*. Close your eyes, open to a random page, plop down a finger. The passage would frequently be uncannily perfect. I watched enough Hammer horror movies with you to know this is the type of ritual that causes the dead to burst out of their grave, especially if a finger happens to get pricked. David Kuhnlein, whom you photographed naked in the mausoleum, wrote, "Kevin then asked me to coax Spicer back from the dead by offering him sex in exchange for a new poem." I wonder if your tours really did awaken something in Spicer. I imagine him alone in the darkness all those years, waiting for exactly what you brought him.

I need to pull together all our financial bits and pieces and turn them over to the capital management firm Erik von Mueller hooked me up with. I need to make a will, to make our literary executors (Andrew Durbin and David Buuck) legal. I need to sell a shitload of books, to get rid of all this art that fills walls, shelves, ledges, drawers, the living room closet, and I imagine much of the storage locker I pay rent on each month with little idea what it contains. Glen is really interested in digging through the boxes, so sometime, probably over summer break, he's going to take stock of it with me. The longer you're dead the grosser it becomes that I own everything—your savings, your 401K, your social security benefits, your ashes. Your stuff is empty without you; it longs to sneak away into a crawl space, to tear itself open to moisture and maggots, to evaporate. It doesn't want me or anybody else fingering it.

With you gone I now own lots of Spicer's stuff too. Rare books, at least one signed letter, that crayon drawing he did that I had hanging beside my bed until indirect sunlight started to fade it. I really don't know what there is—or where it's at. That stack of his canceled checks—did you give them all away or are some still around? I have to stay alive to make sure you and the stuff are secure in your final resting places—mausoleum, archive. From our home to public eyes, public hands. Your memory/legacy will no longer hover in abstraction. There will be a specific place. It has lovely stained glass skylights that are so valuable there've been issues with theft—so if a pilgrim leaves their ID at reception, they'll be allowed to visit you. I don't know if I want to be placed in the niche with you. I have to decide, to account for my name (or not) in the layout of the faceplate, and to order an extra A and a D and a B, a bunch of Es, a V and an R, when we buy the letters for your name. I think I'd rather be tossed into the ocean like Kathy Acker, the wind off the waves blowing my ashes back onto the small group of mourners, flocking them like a Christmas Tree.

I'm walking down Market Street between 9th and 10th, and the sun is squinting bright. Above my sagging mask, my already foggy glasses turn riotous with glare, transforming the bodies that lumber towards me into a mass of silhouettes, flattened, blurred around the edges. I struggle against the sun as the featureless blobs keep approaching, a line of them as far as I can see, relentless in their steady progression—one of them starts shouting with a violence I would normally cross the street to avoid, but the mass won't differentiate enough for me to gauge where/who the danger is, and I panic before the terrible indeterminacy.

When I get home, I watch a video featuring cancelled YouTuber Shane Dawson. It's a big deal since Shane hasn't posted anything for six months. Shane is mourning the sudden death of his kitten, Mario. When the cat passed, Shane felt a warm light in his chest, a golden light that healed all the wounding of being cancelled, and Shane realized that love is the most important thing. He went down to the cat's room, where he got full body chills, and the hair on his arms stood up. Mario came into his life for a reason—he just fucking knew it. Despite his sadness, he felt peace and so much love—and happiness because Mario's soul would always be connected to his. Later, as Shane lay on the couch, holding Mario's little toy, he asked God—or whoever, "Was Mario something else? Was he an angel? Who was he? Is he my guardian angel, is he an angel?" And a voice in his head said, look at the first video, and he went to his phone and looked at the video of the first time he ever saw Mario—in a friend's backyard with the rest of his litter. At the end of the video, all the other kittens are meowing, but Mario's not, and he walks up to an angel statue and just stares at it, and for Shane everything clicked. Mario was saying, yes, I am an angel. Shane will always remember that moment, nobody can tell him it was fake, no one can tell him God doesn't exist, no one can tell him there's nothing after this. He will never ever in his whole life take anything for granted, he will never care about internet comments, he will never care about petty anything. The doubt in the back of his head is gone. "You're a shitty person." "You're not good enough." "Fuck you." All that is gone, and Mario did that.

Shane's breakdown is sad and crazy, and fucking beautiful. I sit at my desk and weep. It's like widow porn. My heart turns sloppy for anyone who's loved enough to grieve. The pain of one widow is the pain of all widows. My optometrist told me that after his father died, all these widow ladies in Chinatown came swooping around his mother with food and invites to group lunch outings. Laura Moriarty said, welcome to the club nobody wants to be a member of, and this past year and a half I've depended on my fellow members, not so much for support, as for recognition. Prageeta. Bruce. Maizie. Laura. Megan. Connie. Hedi. I don't know if any of us believe things happen for a reason. You died because Kaiser was so incompetent they killed you. At the end of a glorious life, a shitstorm.

It's called a cytokine storm—a catastrophic reaction to immunotherapy, resulting in acute respiratory distress syndrome. Meaning your lungs filled with fluid—"ground glass opacities" on the endless x-rays—meaning you couldn't breathe without a ventilator, meaning your organs shut down, meaning decisions needed to be made about whether or not to take you off life support, meaning me. My mother said she had to make that decision for my father and it nearly destroyed her. But my brother said she just whimpered and refused to deal with it, and he was the one who said to pull the plug. Not her. Now that I'm a widow I'm sure that my brother's version is accurate, and I'm sure that my mother didn't lie. There are so many lacunae in my memory, it's like your death and aftermath occurred under a strobe light. Flashes and darkness, flashes and darkness. It's hard to grasp on to any one thing.

On YouTube I watched an interview with the aging Highway Patrol officers who were called to the scene of James Dean's fatal car crash on September 30, 1955. They said there was no evidence that Dean had been drinking or speeding. The driver of the Ford Tudor sedan who crashed into him was also law-abiding and sober. The cops blamed the collision on the silver color of Little Bastard, Dean's Porsche race car, which in the California dusk blended with the highway. The driver of the Ford, who was making a left turn onto a highway on-ramp, didn't see Dean's car. Little Bastard was bleeping in and out of visibility. James Dean was cruising along BLEEP James Dean's neck was broken.

I woke up this morning delighted when my phone screen read Saturday (and not Sunday, like I thought). When it's all screens the distinction between character and live human grows fuzzy like conceptual mildew. Friends, students, and asshole bosses are more interactive than characters, I suppose. I've come to expect—and ask—very little from interactions. Paradoxically, the lower the stakes, the more poignant is any connection. Imagine enduring a yearlong juice fast—solid food—any food—tastes fantastic. It's not just me. For my birthday this year David and I got tacos to go from that place across from the Safeway parking lot, then walked over to the coffee house on the corner of Sanchez and Duboce, got some iced tea, and ate the now lukewarm tacos at the tables on the sidewalk. Across Duboce dogs ran freely in the park. You've been there—a block long stretch of mottled grass and a few trees—David loved it. The nature, the taking off our masks and eating outside—he fantasized bringing his other San Francisco friends there to share the wonders, and he couldn't believe how delicious his shrimp taco was. Isolation had so heightened his senses I imagined he could see the veins on each leaf. He was living in the moment, just like all gurus tell us to, but I felt a twinge of the tragic in what it takes to get a person to the point where so little inspires delight. It took my mother losing everything to discover that I was worthy. She loved me because there was no one else left to love, and I gobbled up her love. David was right; it was a miracle to be sitting there with him. Later that evening, I walked over to the market in the Twitter Building. On my way home, on the corner of Mission and 11th, a man and woman were holding hands. By the time I'd made it to our building, I was crying, I so intensely longed for someone who would care enough for me to hold my hand. I have the eroticism of a child.

Last summer when Will Hall was in the Bay Area visiting his brother, he and I also went to Duboce Park. We sat on a bench drinking coffee and watching the dogs frolic. Will is editing a big collection of your Amazon reviews for Semiotext(e), like 600 pages. You'd love his essay on your *Spreadeagle* art show/novel. There's a kindredness there that surprised me. I see why you asked him to write it. Will told me that Emma Corrin—the actress who played young Princess Diana in Season 4 of *The Crown*—was at Cambridge when he went there, but we lost that thread because this one male dog kept trying to hump another male dog. The distraught owners would separate them, but this dog was determined. Will yelled out, "Hey buddy, that's not the way it works." And I bubbled over with laughter. It's a moment I think about often, the tiniest bleep of joy. My tragic so little. Why didn't I ask him more about Emma Corrin?

The chase chooses clarity over frenzy. No cheesy inserts or cut-aways that take the viewer out of the scene. No maniacal editing. The chase remains coherent, fully inhabiting the primal excitement of the car's physicality, its constant closeness to death. No funny jokes by passengers in the back seat. The camera never leaves the inside of the car. When the audience identifies with someone besides the adrenaline junkie behind the wheel, the chase becomes even more thrilling, more visceral. There's no need for music for the roars, screeches, and slamming of cars make their own music. If there is music, it thumps like a panicky heart.

I don't know if we actually went together or bumped into one another, but I remember seeing John Carpenter-Stephen King's *Christine* with you at the York Theater on 24th Street in the Mission. As an ambassador of female rage, Christine did not disappoint. I remember us sitting in the smoking section and laughing at her evil hijinks. A red and white Plymouth Fury—we both loved King's neon-flashing symbolism. This was 1983, when it would have been unimaginable that in three years we'd be married. From the trailer: *Once she lures you behind the wheel you will be hers, body and soul.* Christine may look like a car but deep down she's a possessive ravenous cunt. Can an object have agency? Or as they put it in the trailer's voiceover: *How do you kill something that can't possibly be alive?* Do objects have power? In witchcraft you move them around to make things happen, you believe. Do objects have feelings? When you throw them out do they weep? We smoked cigarettes and ate greasy popcorn as Christine transformed Arnie from school nerd to punk, her speedometer spinning backwards, her tail fins erect as a demon's ears. Neither of us was attracted to the other, but there was something.

Christine's headlights flare, her windows turn black signaling she is in evil mode, and the chase begins. The camera never enters Christine's interior. It is inaccessible except to our fantasies and an extradiegetic stunt man who peers though a small batch of darkly tinted windshield. He races and crashes with no side or rear vision. When death is on our tail it cannot be seen, only experienced. We run for our lives as Christine's blazing red infests our provincial aesthetics—blood colored jacket, shirt, beer can, lips. In the empty street in front of Dennis' house, the red painted curb gleams like an artery to hell. Out of the darkness Christine's headlights barrel towards us.

After James Dean died, stories about Little Bastard abounded. It—or a car containing any of its parts—kept running into or falling on top of people—crashing into a tree—flipping over. There was a mysterious fire in a warehouse in which it was stored and some suspiciously blown tires, and the guy who tried to steal its steering wheel fell down and gashed his arm. Some fans swear the car is haunted or cursed, that Little Bastard killed James Dean. So, Kevin, what do you think? I imagine a big disembodied eyeroll, similar to the one you'd give when I'd ask why you—who believed so many screwy things—refused to entertain the *possibility* the Kennedys had Marilyn murdered. Joan Didion called her bereavement chronicle *The Year of Magical Thinking*. I'd rename it *The Days of Symbolism Incarnate*. When Rebeca did a psychic reading after Sylvia died, she said Sylvia was hanging out in a tree like a koala. And then I started seeing koalas everywhere. Months later, I'm still seeing them. The distinction between abstract and material has become a joke. I suspect it's always been that way, but in the liminal realm of grief, I keep bumping into it—or it keeps bumping into me. No divide between animate and animation. A human sits at a piano, his fingers banging out something lively, and a musical staff swoops up from the keyboard in a wave, its notes bopping about with glee.

There were sixteen Christines used for filming, seven more for parts. When the movie wrapped, only two remained drivable. They went on a promotional tour, while Christine's sacrificial sisters were send to a lot and sold for $20 a carload. Always there is the crisis of remnants. I don't think I'll ever crawl out from under all the art and books you left behind—your collection of tiny ceramic figurines that are baked into French cakes—John Water's glass Christmas ornament with the cockroach inside. I can't just have it all hauled away; I have to sort the rare, the valuable, the sentimental from the junk; catalogue it; contact experts. And then there's my own shopaholic excess. Before COVID, people would come over and help me go through it all. People would touch our objects, place them in new arrangements, take some away, but never enough. To relax I watch decluttering videos on YouTube, but those perky moms with their hacks for establishing order in a kitchen drawer never touch my situation. Just like in the movie, some fan pieced together a complete Christine from all the smashed up leftovers, and his Frankensteined car is now said to be worth a million dollars. I feel like a princess or a peasant wandering through an enchanted forest, tasked with choosing that which is of true value. My head is fuzzy. The air is thick, difficult to navigate. As I drive to Andronico's at night, overhead lights look like an amusement park ride. It's like I'm drifting through a dream in my little Yaris bubble.

You received a letter in the mail today, hand-addressed with jaunty circles for the dots over the I's. "SF" instead of San Francisco, just like a local. No return address. I wondered, who would send something this personal who wouldn't know you were dead. I had soap opera visions of a lost lover or sibling or illegitimate child announcing they were ready to change your life forever. I opened it with trepidation—what if the Kevin I knew was not the Kevin inside the envelope? If anybody could lead a secret second life and not get discovered, it would be you, and I thought back to your youthful predilection for having sex with married men and how you hypothesized that was the reason that you, whose partners were in the four-figure range, didn't contract HIV. One time, looking back at those days, you said excitedly that you were now a married man yourself, as if it were the kinkiest of positions. The letter turned out to be Christian spam from a woman named Karen. She included a booklet entitled "Can the dead really live again?" The answer: It's not like Jehovah hasn't resurrected people before. 1 Corinthians 15:26: "The last enemy that shall be destroyed is death."

On your birthday this year, I guess it would have been your 68th, I was on a five-day juice fast. I imagined how you would roll your eyes at that—a major motif of our togetherness—your rolling your eyes at my kooky New Age ways—details of which frequently found their way into your poems. The pattern was: make fun of the wife then harvest her weirdness. The two-beat rhythm of our generative love. Preparing for the Sylvia Plath class I taught in the fall, I found it painful to read about her relationship with Ted—not the breakup part but the glory days of them writing together, inspiring one another—two lovers inebriated with language. Your favorite poems, the real showstoppers, such as "Who," I must have heard you read a couple dozen times, and I never stopped being awed. When you died you were gone. Instantly. Gone. No whoo-whoo hovering presence or guidance for the grieving widow. The internet claimed many sightings, a flashing light they knew was you, etc. But the only time I feel your presence is in your writing—your quirkiness, your sly intensity as you pull out the rug from beneath the reader's feet. From "Cat Scan":

> You lie on your back, flimsy gown of paper,
> and a cat walks down your body,
> your forehead, your throat, sternum, stomach
> and so forth, til the tiptoeing creature stares
> back at you over his shoulder.
> Kevin, you are going to die.

I love the cartoony beginning, and how without warning, the poem ends by slamming itself into a wall. I heard you read those cat poems a lot—they were favorites of mine—but when I stumbled upon them in your manuscripts folder on the computer, I was apprehensive. *Kevin, you are going to die*. Rebeca said that when Sylvia passed you were there to greet her, but I don't know. You never liked Sylvia all that much.

This year I spent Thanksgiving alone, planning to toss off a letter to you, a couple of pages at the most. I kept thinking back to our first public appearance together as a couple—the huge Thanksgiving dinner we co-hosted at your place on Guerrero Street. We spent like $100 on groceries, which was exorbitant in the early '80s. I cooked a turkey and the gravy, and the surprised gaze of our friends added a whole new layer of sexy. I imagined us creating a home of love and warmth, with a slew of visitors who would bask in that warmth. We had so much love, it was too much for just the two of us—we had to share it with the world. Exactly the life you wanted at the end, and which I resisted. Instead it was Kevin the beneficent and Dodie, jealous of the short time we had left, futilely trying to slam the door in the face of all those intruders. It was like a zombie movie—I'd get rid of one and another would pop up in its place. You made each person feel so special, they seemed to think they had as much right to you as I. You were always gregarious, but this was something else, it was like a transmutation, like your self was effervescing, dispersing among the masses. I imagine death for you as a further dispersal, the zillion droplets of yourself greeting the angels. I don't know if this was a spiritual enlightenment or an effect of your brain tumor or both. I tried to be a selfless caretaker but I've always been a horrible wife—moody and combustible, flipping back and forth between ignoring you and whining for attention. I never took the garbage out, I didn't read the final version of your novel *Spreadeagle*. Not only did I fuck other people, I fell in love with them—all that was fine, you said, as long as when things turned to shit you didn't have to take care of me, and then you took care of me anyway. The last thing you wanted was a good wife. The unspoken promise of our partnership was that neither of us would ever have to be "normal." We would be two misfits saving one another.

In my dream it is easy to tell the dead from the living. The living are full color, whereas the dead are black and white. While still asleep, I'm aware I'm dreaming in a movie cliché. I am given two wishes. My first is that you were still alive. The second is that the cats could talk.

I stream every Christian Petzold film I can access. The plot begins when a car goes off the road and lands in a body of water. It ends with a car hurling off an ocean cliff and crashing on the shore below. In my journal I write: subconscious drives. I know you don't care for foreign movies unless they have Isabelle Huppert in them because she's a real star. But Nina Hoss—Petzold's favorite—is pretty fabulous, in that repressed, gaunt, no ass or tits to speak of, German way. Playing around on Ancestry.com I discovered that my German immigrant great grandfather was really from Poland, that his surname wasn't Hoff, it was Hnat. Joseph Hnat, his father Onufri Hnat. Mary Jane, my mother's cousin, who I've corresponded with, says it was all about anti-Polish sentiment. I wrote back—no wonder I've always loved stuffed cabbages—it's in my DNA. I'm reminded of joking with my brother at my mom's funeral, that if this were a soap, a unknown sibling would appear, and Joey said, "You do have a sister." I think about her often. I doubt if even a private eye could find her. She's from Michigan City and was conceived before my parents were married. She's always there, a vague double who could materialize at any moment. I think of how amused you were when Lydia Lunch moved to San Francisco, and the ensuing rivalry between her and Kathy. You'd declare with a big smile, "There's only room for one Kathy Acker at the San Francisco Art Institute—and now there's two!" When I was in college my sister rang my parents' doorbell, and my father told her—in his blue collar obscenity-riddled manner—to go away and not come back. Nobody bothered to tell Joey her name. I don't know what's crueler, my father or the limits of my knowing. When I walk from the kitchen to the back porch, I hear a bird screech just like the birds in *Yella*, which Petzold, borrowing from *Carnival of Souls*, used to announce the transition between the land of the living and the land of the dead. For a moment I worry my vision will switch and I'll enter an altered world.

> Q: Why do they play on artificial turf in Poland?
> A: To keep the cheerleaders from grazing.

On YouTube I saw Kylie Minogue in a clip from a talk show with Josh O'Connor and Emma Corrin—young Charles and young Diana on Season 4 of *The Crown*. I thought Corrin was miscast. She's a shrimp for one thing, and most of her character development seemed to be about tilting her head to the side and making very un-Diana-like bug eyes. But everybody loved her, and Kylie was sitting there with her huge sparkling smile—clearly her segment preceded this and she was there just to respond and fill up space. Kylie has a new album out. It's called *Disco*. People have been posting song videos on Facebook, in your honor. I've avoided listening to any of it. With Kylie I have no defenses. All I can think about is the ICU. One of the graphs on the machines you were hooked up to was dangerously high or low, and as soon as I started playing Kylie, it moved toward stability. You really did love her. The nurse was stunned this was your favorite music. Reassessment dramatically swept across her face, as if she were the heroine in a silent film. Suddenly you were more than just this old guy who got the short end of the stick, and she was curious. Even while unconscious you had the power to impress.

I text Will and ask him to finish his story about Emma Corrin at Cambridge. His response is lackluster: "Haha, there's not much of a story. She studied languages, kept a low profile. She was a low key type as far as I can tell. Who knew she was off doing important modeling and acting in London on the side! Not the kind of girl that you would see in the cafeteria and say, wow, that's a star, but maybe I wasn't paying enough attention . . . and maybe that's the Diana type?" Once again, my fantasy of what I've been missing is more vivid than the real thing. And now my mind is tripping off into all the ways I took you for granted, and I rationalize that nobody could be together long-term without taking one another for granted. Endless intensity is claustrophobic. You were the most loving, kind person I've ever met. And the most amoral. I remember you saying early on, there is no such thing as a good relationship or a bad relationship. There's just relationship. From you I learned that radical amorality is the key to loving. The refusal to judge. Vision of you exclaiming, "She's *terrible!*" with a gleam on your face, as if you'd encountered a great prima donna. I wonder what you would have made of Emma Corrin in the cafeteria at St. John's College. You used to say that movie stars tend to be short with big heads because the camera loves them. Gore Vidal called them "the little people, who were like dolls until properly lit and told to move about in that nine-foot-square area where the photoplay had its cramped limited life." It makes perfect sense they didn't cast a lanky Diana, all Cubist angles topped with a poufy shag.

You had a really big head yourself. Hats never fit you.

I read that Corrin is taller than she looked on screen—5'8". Maybe it's because—as I'm sure you were well aware—the real Charles and Diana were exactly the same height—5'10". Due to her un-princesslike proportions, real Diana was required to wear flats and short heels, and in official photos, the couple was always staged to make Charles look taller. Corrin looks like an official photo rather than the abject, hunched-over Diana. I've been 5'6" since I was eleven, when I towered over the other children. My mother said in horror that at the rate I was growing I'd end up six feet tall or worse. I used to read magazine articles about procedures where they could cut out part of your bones to make you look like a normal female. I stop for a moment to take in the colors of the room—pearlescent pink of fountain pen, neon orange silicone mat, peacock blue curtains patterned with metallic gold dots, saturated yellow external hard drive box, bright navy rim of white enameled bowl. It doesn't matter what I look at for splendor has been abstracted from use value. I'm reminded of driving to San Francisco State, my car tunneling through trees and ever-changing skies, and me thinking—this is the tragedy of death, that I will never again see *this*, a throwaway moment. Driving is when I cry for you, Nick Cave on the CD player. All the other CDs have been stolen, so I play the same one over and over, disk two from *Ghosteen*.

While I'm waiting for the Novocaine to kick in, the dentist tells me a story about a friend. Behind his mask and face shield his voice is muffled, so like a cat I listen to his tone for comfort, clueless to the content. Afterwards, I walk down Sanchez, sipping insanely hot and sweet chai. No matter how I adjust my mask my glasses fog, so I take them off and totter along. Everything looks blurry, as if Vaseline has been smeared over the lens for a cheap flashback sequence. Just as I think this, I approach Books and Bookshelves and remember that reading Marsha Campbell gave there back in the '80s—I think she was living there for a while—and the piece she read was about how when the store was closed she'd check out the titles of books that were lying around unshelved, and decipher the secret messages the staff was leaving for her—all of them abusive. Did Marsha greet you on the other side? So far our New Narrative anthology has done little to immortalize her. She remains dead and unknown, a schizophrenic woman who lived in an SRO and starred in the free writing workshops offered to San Francisco's homeless—and open mics, where she was infamous for sleeping with all those gnarly guys who read poems scrawled on scraps of paper. Due to Amazon and self-publishing, most of them now have books they relentlessly promote. Nothing is pure any more. Marsha was brilliant, endlessly inventive, shocking, with an ability to reconfigure disparate bits of data that made me jealous. Her mind was vast and puffy and shifting as the clouds that thrilled my childhood, when I had nothing better to do than lie on my back and stare at the sky. The spirits of all the writers we've known who have passed over, are you with them? Do they care who's reading their books, who's organizing a paranoid landscape based on their titles alone? Does it do any good to honor the dead? Does the author's spirit depart from the writing, as it does from the body? Or do the words hold an indelible spark? I don't touch your books, but I open files on the computer, and you are so present in the words your departure feels impossible.

At Market I turn right and head towards Castro. A gym has moved its machines onto the sidewalk. Friday afternoon, less than a week into our second lockdown. There is only one guy on the gym part of the sidewalk. He's lying on his back, knees in the air—and he's balancing a tiny barbell on his groin as he thrusts his hips in the air then back down to the ground, up and down up and down and suddenly I'm missing you. I'm sure you'd have an opinion about what was going on here, you who wrote about sex kinks I'd never heard of, rosary beads up the asshole, pull them out slowly, one by one. What do you think? Is the guy getting off on this bar bell groin thing? Or did his trainer put him up to it? Is he pumping up his fucking muscles? Thrust up, thrust down, I wonder how long he'll keep going—it's frustrating that I can't just stand and gape, that I have to keep on walking like I have somewhere to go. I see so few 3-D humans these days—it's frustrating I can't pause him, can't rewind, can't even cheer him on. Go you superfucker, go! I'm reminded of a story about a toddler who had been raised playing on an iPad, and so the child was looking at an image in a print magazine, and they placed the tips of their thumb and pointer finger on the picture and spread them wide, then brought them back together and spread them across the picture again, looking confused, until the adults in this story realized the child was trying to zoom the magazine image, that they didn't understand that all of life couldn't be zoomed. After a year in isolation, I get it. The rules of the material world seem increasingly tentative. The few times a week I leave the apartment and enter the material world, I seem to glide through it, feet barely touching the ground, head swiveling from side to side. There's little interacting. I'm like a ghost. I'm like you. Do you have any special powers? Can you see into peoples' hearts, zap across dimensions? Do you silently flap through the night, your bright wings reflecting the moon, stunning the creatures who scuttle in the forest below?

When I return home my heart opens. This happens frequently, erratically. Imagine a time-lapse film of a bud twirling open into full bloom. My open heart feels floppy; gladly would it brush against anything, anybody. When I told Peter Gizzi that grieving had been good for his writing, he said it gave him a soul.

Why did you have to go? It's intolerable you left and with such a brutal end. Most lung cancer victims—I read somewhere—die not of lung cancer but of infections or reactions to chemo. I was eager to take on your dying, to totally devote myself to your sickness. It's as if this hidden cave in my psyche opened and out flew a swarm of bats wearing little nurse's caps. No decision was involved; my drive to care for you was instinctual as those Monarch butterflies we saw that one Thanksgiving day in Santa Cruz, which traveled vast distances to roost in those specific trees, their branches all aflutter, the limbs of an Ovidian god-beast. My urge to care repelled you, who were all about extracting the last dregs from life, who were ravenous to live and live and live, hobbling and racing around with the cane Kaiser gave you because of all the blood thinners—if you fell down it would have been disastrous—you didn't give a fuck about my research into chemo side effects. The bag of quick dissolving mints I bought that are supposed to help with nausea, you wouldn't touch them. When we first met, your stories/memoirs about your self-destructive youth terrified me, though I loved the writing. Your past felt surreal, like nobody was behind the wheel and you were careening. Everybody who knew you when you were young agrees—and you affirmed this yourself, repeatedly—that I saved your life, that you would have been dead long ago without me.

The chase scene has begun. You sit upright on the edge of the couch, your attention absolutely fixed on the TV. None of that messy here and there/in and out/past and present. You are right here right now, watching with the focused precision of a laser sight on a Smith & Wesson, registering waves of awe, terror, delight. Your face fragments and coalesces like a claymation character, a series of ever-moving parts that twitch and bulge, revealing emotion. Grunts, gasps, laughter, inrush and outrush of excited breathing. As the world rushes in through your eyes and ears, our living room becomes the cab of the car. You're buckled in, careening into a dangerous future.

Your hospital room was so packed with visitors I had to leave. Your friends were possessive—and at the end when I put my foot down—no, this is about family now—it was a battle. Some people couldn't conceive there could be a private Kevin space they couldn't access, so fully you seemed to have given yourself to them. You would have been a better widow than I. You'd suffered bravely and sentimentally—far and wide—your widowhood would inspire people, bring them together—you would convince even those who hated me in life that in death I was a saint. And then the masses, ravenous for the kindness and generosity you perfected over the thirty-three years I was married to you—from quirky, unrelatable drunk to charismatic daddy you arose, capable of melting the hardest of hearts—could absorb you.

You knew to revere the dead. You wrote that finding where Spicer was buried satisfied "a huge longing in my own heart because, as I hope you have seen, for a man like me there's no closure unless I go to the grave and fall down on it, as I did to John Ford's grave in Holy Cross Cemetery in Culver City, and embrace spectral memory as a living thing in my arms." On the bathroom wall hangs the snapshot you took of Frank O'Hara's grave that one time we were visiting your parents in Smithtown and took a trip to the Green River Cemetery in Springs. *Grace to be born and live as variously as possible.* Online I look at photos of O'Hara's funeral, July 27, 1966. Allen Ginsberg on a dirt path, head cast down, arm around the shoulders of Kenneth Koch. Women in flats and low heels, one wearing an era-iconic paisley sheath. Handsome Bill Berkson in a suit. I read about the "violent eulogy, full of raw fury" delivered by O'Hara's sometimes lover Larry Rivers, in which he describes O'Hara's destroyed body in graphic detail. Mourners groaned and yelled, "Stop! Stop!" O'Hara's mother gasped. The text of the eulogy is almost impossible to find. I googled and googled and googled and finally in a YouTube video artist Skylar Fein reads it. Here's my notes: His skin was purple where it showed through the white gown—his body was a quarter larger than usual—sewing every few inches, some stitches straight, three or four inches long—some stitches semi-circular and longer—eyes receded into head, lids black—quick gasps of breath—whole body quivered—tube in nostrils—he looked like a shaped wound—leg bone broken, splintered, piercing the skin, every rib cracked—a third of his liver wiped out. Rivers: "What good can talking about it do? I don't know." To my widow self this is poetry. The bereaved clings to all the tender details of dying. When you've seen the unseeable, there's no easy return. Nothing else makes sense.

Here's a timeline of what happened to you:

January 1, 2019: You officiate the wedding of Aaron and Jackie. This is the last time we dared pretend things were normal. You were shuffling and unstable but you hadn't started falling down. Early/mid February: Primary care physician diagnoses you with sleep apnea. From a February 17 email you wrote to your sister Maureen:

The weird thing is that for the last six weeks or so, or maybe since Christmas, I've been feeling a lot of strange physical ailments—and I've gone to Kaiser to find out what's going on. One of them involves not being able to type anymore, not like I used to. It's like my fingers can't find the right keys and it slows me down, way down. It's almost like I had a stroke but the doctor confirms I had no stroke! Right now I'm messaging you through a dictation software that Dodie found for me online, which has been a godsend, since I have been used to writing everyday for all these years, and now I'm like a savage who never saw a keyboard before. It takes me, like, five minutes to complete a single sentence, mostly getting rid of typos heehee. So frustrating.

I feel like I'm out of balance in general between the two halves of my body left and right. When I walk I have a pronounced limp, usually in my right leg but sometimes in both legs! Nothing makes sense, but there may be a light at the end of the tunnel. My doctor suspects I have sleep apnea! I scoffed at that because I've always been able to sleep on a dime. But I went for the test: they have you sleep attached to a machine for four hours, and I thought I was sleeping through the whole thing, but the nurse said I had 73 brief wake ups because I ran out of oxygen each time! The doctor tells me that if you have more than 30 such interruptions then you have a severe case of apnea: he spelled "severe" in all capital letters—scary—but now I'm taking him seriously.

February 22: The first reference in my journal that something was up with you: "Kevin coming back this evening. He seems okay so far." You flew alone to give a reading at UMass Amherst. March 7: We fly to Bellingham, give a reading at Western Washington University, go to the opening of our joint art show at Hardware Applied Services, then drive to Vancouver for a 2-day poet's theater workshop and performance. March 9: Karen Tallman hosts a party, where we reunite with all the aging Vancouver poets (George Bowering, Fred Wah, George Stanley, Meredith and Peter Quartermain, and many more) and I think (and I'm not the only one) *this is the last time these people will ever gather together.* Karen tells me stories of her childhood interactions with Jack Spicer. April 5: You visit my primary care physician, who immediately orders an MRI. (No MRI appointments available until April 22.) Dr. Strako tells you never to return to your other doctor, and that it's too dangerous to travel. She can't assure you that you will be okay. We cancel our May trip to New York. April 9: You are doing so poorly, I cancel my April 16 reading at Gallery 400 in Chicago. April 15: Ambulance takes you to Kaiser San Francisco ER. April 16: Ambulance takes you to Kaiser Redwood City Neurosurgery Department (spa-like second honeymoon). April 20: San Francisco Kaiser Hospital (grungy with overworked resentful nurses; you ask priest to pray for you—me, Peter Maravelis, Bradford cry). May 1–3: Three targeted radiation treatments to your brain with the CyberKnife, Kaiser South San Francisco (scary waiting room but interior with lovely slatted blond wood walls), where they pipe in Kylie Minogue during your treatments. Happy steroid times. May 29: You perform in your play *Box of Rain* at the Stud. You can't make it up the stage stairs, so you stand at the front of the audience and deliver your lines. May 30: We attend the John Waters reading/interview at McRoskey Mattress Company. June 7: One round of chemo and immunotherapy, Kaiser Ambulatory Care, San Francisco. Six hours later, ambulance to ER, admission to Kaiser ICU. A couple days later, priest gives you last rights, which makes your Catholic-school-scarred sisters livid. June 15: Another priest reads "Litany of the Saints," with your sisters and me responding. Priest: *Holy Mary.* Maureen, Nancy and I: *Pray for us.* Priest: *Saint Kevin.* Maureen, Nancy and I: *Pray for us.* Everybody cries. You listen to Kylie Minogue on my phone as you die (Kylie Essentials playlist on iTunes).

August 25: Hundreds attend your 3-hour memorial at SFMOMA. The Phyllis Wattis Theater and a spillover room with a livestream were not enough to hold them all. Many were turned away. Bradford was in charge of it, and he was amazing. The audience cried, but they were entertained. Afterwards people said it was the best memorial they'd ever been to. You would have loved it, especially the staging of a scene from your play *Stagefright*, when your great stars of the 1990s, Phoebe Gloeckner and Michelle Rollman, returned to stun us. Thank god Katy stayed with me that weekend. I don't think I would have managed to get dressed and make it there. We took the Mission Street bus.

I wake to a GoFundMe plea to support Kat Harrison. I met her just a few weeks after you died, when I drove up to Occidental for the weekend with Bett Williams and her girlfriend. It was a spontaneous trip. I dreamt about Bett or she dreamt about me, and I texted or called her, and she invited me to come along with them. In person, you'd be wanting to know the name of Bett's girlfriend. If you didn't know someone's name it made you anxious. Beth, the girlfriend is Beth. I think Kat was supposed to give a lecture on psychedelic mushrooms, but it got cancelled. This was so soon after you died, when my mind was still a sticky thing that bits stuck to, random bits. I have no complete pictures. The talk was canceled but we went anyway. Bett drove our Yaris and Beth drove with their four dogs in the van they sleep in when they travel. Occidental is in Sonoma County, half an hour drive west of Santa Rosa. It's this adorable hippie touristy place, with cozy bars and coffee houses, good non-fussy food, live music. The air felt supercharged with oxygen from the surrounding redwood forests and the sense of community the locals exhibited, a commonality I longed to dissolve in, given my recent shock of aloneness. If a place could wrap its arms around you and give you a hug, that's what Occidental felt like.

The three of us had breakfast with Kat, then Bett and I met with her at Botanical Dimensions, the ethnobotanic library she founded. Ethnobotany is an anthropological approach to botany, how various cultures use medicinal plants and mushrooms. Lots about mushrooms. Kat used to be married to Terrence McKenna, who was not a good husband. Kat and Bett knew one another from the psychedelic community, which they gossiped about with abandon. I was stunned and amused how the hijinks of the psychedelic community so parallels shit that goes down in the poetry community. I got this image of all these microcosms across the globe that are considered discrete yet somehow manage to totally mirror one another. Kat, who is in her early '70s with soft white hair, is lowkey and focused; I instantly wanted to sidle up to her. I was disappointed I have no interest in psychedelics but she's a writer, so there was that.

Sometime later that weekend the three of us went for a walk among the redwoods. We got up really close to Kat's favorite trees; we stood inside them, sharing the darkness with bats and god knows what other crawling creatures. Kat pointed out their burn marks and sworls; she told us miraculous things about the trees I no longer remember—she reminded me of a docent in a museum, she reminded me of you, my personal docent. The trees are frequently struck by lightning, or at least Kat's favorite trees were—their physiognomy forever altered by seemingly random attacks. She said the trees were all connected, were really one organism—if one tree is in trouble other trees share something or other—I don't remember the details—to help it out. I imagined the forest floor as an expansive nervous system, the soles of my feet vibrating with electrified tree currents. When we walked back to our cars, Kat gave me a long stalk of mugwort from her garden—not the kind you would buy in a store, indigenous mugwort—and she said that it would help me with what I was "going through." At home I put it on the door of the closet where your ashes sit, to calm and protect you.

So on my iPhone I read that in mid-January this guy suffering from meth-induced psychosis broke down Kat's front door, smashed up her dining room, and strangled her. Thankfully a neighbor heard her screams and chased the guy off. He's since been caught and charged with attempted murder. He's a local. I gave $50 to her GoFundMe. Do you think I should have given more? They raised $72,000 in two days. We raised over $40,000 to place your ashes in the same room as Jack Spicer's. The last time I went to Cypress Lawn—with Wayne Smith and Cris Bell—it was late in the afternoon, and the light was quickly fading. It grew so dark beneath the saturated greens and reds of the stained glass skylights, we had to use the flashlights on our phones to see. It was creepy, like horror movie creepy. The GoFundMe page is titled Help Kat Harrison Recover from Violence. I think of all the crazy ranting men I have skirted around in San Francisco, and now with COVID and all the business closures and fleeing techies and lack of tourists to rob, I'm afraid to go out at night, even to park my car a couple of blocks away. Routinely I fantasize escaping to someplace slower and drenched in Nature, someplace safe. Even though Kat knew who the guy was, the attack is considered random. It feels like a curse, like a thick black X over the heart of paradise. Recently the mugwort disappeared. I don't know what happened to it.

There is no aloneness in the redwood forest's communal web. Lightning strikes an elder and the other trees rush in to save her.

After his son died, Nick Cave opened himself to a larger sense of love and started a newsletter. When someone you love dies, that love shatters and flies out into a larger world. I'm not looking for your replacement. I'm looking to explode my concept of love, to disperse it. In other words, to be more like you.

Your address "book" was an MS Word file formatted for two columns. When someone died you typed DEAD, in all caps bold, beside their name. A wise choice for the biographer in you—future scholars need to know addresses. But, more importantly, the DEAD was a marker, a remembrance. In your heart the dead didn't leave, they just changed form. The In Memorium was your favorite segment of the Oscars. You looked forward to crying during it. You had no shame about crying during movies. That's what they were for. In 2017, Jennifer Moxley asked you to help her pull together an In Memoriam for poets, to be presented at the upcoming National Poetry Foundation conference at the University of Maine. It had been five years since the previous conference, and lots of poets had died. You were great as master of ceremonies, and your Oscar-styled slideshow of poets' heads and emotional music was a big hit at that year's lobster banquet—except for the killjoys who kept coming up with dead poets you folks had left out. Now I'm thinking of the first National Poetry Foundation conference we went to—I'm pretty sure it was 1996. Stephen King showed up at the lobsterfest, and all those poets and academics acted like it was no big deal, but you were ready for him, with a stack of his novels and your autograph book sequestered in your bag. That horrible photo of the three of us, King in the middle, your huge smile on one side, and me on the other, my hair hennaed bright red and my bangs disastrously self-cut, all raggedy and uneven. It looks like I've been attacked by a pair of demonic scissors.

The rent and COBRA payments were a couple of days overdue, something that never would happen on your watch, but the retro tedium of writing checks, copying receipts, stuffing sealing addressing and stamping envelopes destroys me. All the other bills are on autopay, or I enter a few numbers online and click PAY. I always walk the checks over to the post office, enlivened by my full body immersion in natural light and weather. After the post office I planned to walk back to the car (which needed to be moved for street cleaning; I haven't gotten a ticket in at least three months!) and drive to Rainbow for white wine, vegan mozzarella, lemons, and the ingredients I was missing to recreate the Singapore Noodles from the YouTube cooking video I watched a couple of days ago. So I get to the corner of 11th and Mission, and across the street is this guy without a shirt who is yelling and gyrating and pacing. I immediately thought of Kat's meth-fueled psychotic, and the terror of her attack hit me, like I was having a flashback that was not my own—bursts of violence, not so much images as jabs of homicidal energy. The guy on the corner showed no control over his jagged motions, weaving and jerking all over the sidewalk, snarl-shouting, but in general he seemed to be heading towards Van Ness. So I crossed 11th towards 10th, then suddenly he was heading towards 10th as well—I don't know how he got there so quickly—it's as if he were moving through time and space in blips. *Shards of wood and glass, fingers digging into neck flesh.* Halfway across 11th I turned and went back to the corner. He was heading in the exact route I'd been planning. I remembered reading about this asshole in Alabama who got arrested for feeding a caged squirrel meth in order to turn it into an attack squirrel. The squirrel was really vicious, poor thing. That's what this guy was like, a drugged-up attack squirrel, his quick frantic gestures an attempt to shake off whatever was happening inside his body.

I decided to move the car to this rare spot I noticed next to the Aikido Studio (now closed and boarded up), and then walk to Rainbow. The car was on Natoma in the cul de sac, and halfway there I see the guy in the distance, flailing and heading in the direction of Rainbow—but just sort of. His ragged blond hair and taut unhealthy shirtless torso made me think of Axl Rose at the height of his "Knocking on Heaven's Door" fame. Miraculously the space next to the Aikido Studio was still there. I lock the car—scan for danger—walk toward a neighborhood mailbox—scan each intersection—deposit checks—scan for danger—head down 12th towards Folsom and Rainbow. At the end of that long block there's a gyrating figure. The guy is so frenetic my telescopic vision easily locks in on him. He's stomping and kicking, his thighs and calves bent at right angles, his arms bent as well. His limbs never seem to straighten out as he does his loose-limbed hopping. He looks like a choreomaniacal skeleton in a Medieval painting. He is why I hardly leave the house anymore. I no longer have you to walk me to the car, to speed dial if anything scary should happen.

I turned around and in front of the residency hotel, two guys were talking amicably. The one with his back to me had light colored pants that were encrusted with shit. Of course I thought of Samuel Delany's fetishization of shit in *The Mad Man*, and how he used to live in the neighborhood. This week I watched a video of a dialogue between Delany, Jackie Wang, and Huw Lemmey in which Delany calculated that he'd had sex with 50,000 people. He goes out every other day and does twelve people a day and he's ancient, etc. He makes it sound so natural, sweet even. Unlike the honed algorithms of dating apps, Delany's random analogue sex is full of surprises. He gets excited by bodies and acts he never dreamed of. From samueldelany.com: *Hacker, Caruso, and now Delany were living in a sprawling 2nd-floor flat at*

1067 Natoma St. upstairs from a black woman named Helen, who claimed to be a witch. When I Google Map it, it's in the cul de sac, right where my car had been parked. The flat is now a condo. On May 21, 2019 it sold for $1,500,000. Samueldelany.com continues: *At the Green Valley Restaurant, toward the top of Green St. in North Beach in 1969, George Stanley told Delany, "You have confused the true and the real." Marilyn, William Alvin Moore (then, Bill Brodecky), and possibly Paul Caruso were also present.*

Kevin, there is so much here you could unpack for me. The Bill Brodecky connection is a surprise. I don't know why. I do a search for his name in your Spicer Folder on the computer, and the links to Delany are all over the place. I open a file containing Delany's not-for-circulation remarks following the New York celebration of the release of Spicer's collected poems. I guess both of us were on a panel with him. He initially refers to me as "Dody Bellamy (Kevin's wife and a very nice person)." But when he gets to my presentation he writes, "Alas, Bellamy's not a good reader." "Fucker," I huff. Brodecky's the one who painted the Nancy Drew covers. There was a huge one hanging in some room at that party we went to the day after I had the panic attack, and even though we hardly knew one another I spent the night in your bed. You fixed me a cup of warm milk, and you held me and told me the plot of Stephen King's novella *The Mist*, and I was surprised that anybody could calm me down like that, especially you. Standing in front of floor-to-ceiling Nancy Drew, for the first time I felt awkward with you, not knowing what to do with this intimacy that had happened to us. Like the difference between the true and the real, it was a mystery I couldn't wrap my mind—or heart—around. Another mystery: that time you pulled out a pair of manicure scissors and took a snip of Delany's long gray beard and placed it in a Ziploc bag—why did you do it? We were in a bar on Valencia, after his reading at Modern Times. Of course he agreed, he's so *say yes to life*. When you knew you were dying you told person after person that you led the exact life you wanted. You'd add with a big smile, "How many people can say that?" *The servant vanished, to reappear a few minutes later with a sparkling ornament on a purple velvet cushion. Nancy drew in her breath.* How did meth guy get to 12th and Folsom so fast? In the 3-D world, too many surprises.

I have to switch insurance carriers because an encounter with Kaiser—even driving past the hospital—sets off flashes of the week-long grind to your terrible death, a death I had to authorize. I asked your sisters what they thought we should do, and neither would offer an opinion. I was the wife. It was on me alone. At first I had them turn off all life support except the breathing tube. Dr. Strako said you should last a day, but two days later your vitals were stronger than when we began. Maybe I should have taken that as a sign you weren't ready to go. On *Grey's Anatomy* they're always pulling people back from the brink of death. And then there's those articles about COVID, where people's lungs fill up just like yours did with whatever it is lungs fill with, auto-immune reaction gunk, but when their organ systems start shutting down, the doctors keep them alive anyway. So maybe you could have survived. People tell me I should avoid thoughts like these. *Okay, for sure, I'll just jump right on that avoiding.* One thing I learned in my week sitting beside your bed in the ICU is that doctors tell you what they want you to hear, and they made it seem tortuous to leave you in your condition, drugged unconscious, organ systems shutting down, opportunistic infections setting in. Finally, I agreed—take out the tube—and I sat there and held you and watched you expire. Did you watch along with me, hovering with your back to the ceiling, looking down at my messily parted skull? Did you shout out: "What's happening?" "Why is no one responding to me?" Then finally: "Wife-woman, let go." You were textbook Irish, a drunk and a super storyteller. And even though you didn't go to Mass, the most Catholic person I ever met. I hope your last rites worked, I hope that you're walking along a golden path with Jesus and Terry Black, who you loved as a boy and who died of AIDS before the book you wrote about him was published. I hope the tree that Sylvia's sitting in is hanging over that path.

When you became incapable of typing, I figured out the computer's dictation software and showed you how to use it. When you were having trouble putting on your shoes, I bought you an extra-long shoe horn. Even though you walked with an unsteady shuffle, refusing my offer of a cane, you flew to Amherst alone in the dead of winter, where you fell down on the ice. Your state was so distressing, Peter worried you had ALS, like his brother. We later learned you had an aneurism, and you could have died on the plane. When you went to my doctor the first thing she did was order an MRI, but at Kaiser it takes weeks to get one. You started falling down, always when I wasn't around. More than once it took you 45 minutes to get back up. Friends said I should take you to the ER and throw a fit, that they'd give you an MRI right away, but you didn't consider yourself an emergency. Friends kept insisting, and I said, "He doesn't want to go. He's not a child." I didn't tell them that when I tried to push you, you'd get panicky and start crying. Friends said that in this instance I needed to treat you like a child. You kept getting worse and it was all on me, my bad caring. Then one morning you woke me in tears because you couldn't dress yourself so I got up and helped, and then a couple of hours later on the phone you said it was too difficult to function and if I'd pick you up after work, you'd go to the ER. I had ordered a Vegetarian Delight lunch special at Red Jade when someone from your office called and said you collapsed and were in an ambulance. When I got to the ER

I walked past dozens of people in the waiting room, showed my ID to the guard, and found you, conscious and stable, waiting for some test result. I joked that you staged the whole thing so you could skip the horrible line in the waiting room. All these details go thud thud thud. Who cares about them.

When they left you and me alone to "decide" if you should be intubated they didn't tell us that meant they'd drug you unconscious for days, that you might never talk again, that those who undergo intubation have more than twice the mortality risk of other ICU patients. The two most common things for loved ones to say to the patient before their intubation: "I love you." "I hope you do well." We foolishly thought we had agency, when in fact we were in a well-trod maze, the hospital staff directing us, step by step. You said anything was better than the mask that was forcing oxygen down your throat—anything. Love beaming from your eyes you said, "We had a good long run of it, didn't we?" You said it wasn't enough, we needed more. We hadn't yet learned that in the ICU there is always something worse. I had to leave the room and they closed the curtains and it took hours. They wouldn't let me inside, so eventually I went out to dinner.

Online I read that unless there are problems, the process shouldn't take more than five minutes. What the hell did you go through behind that curtained glass wall? I stay up all night, until 7 or 8 in the morning reading about what could go wrong with an intubation. A lot—dangerously low blood oxygen levels, cardiac arrest, nasty brain stuff. The level 5 sedation drugs they gave you are common, but I can't tell if they were standard procedure or crisis management. Machines monitored your heart rhythm, your temperature, your blood oxygen levels and many more processes the nurses didn't tell me about. Sometimes I forgot to pay attention to you, the digital readouts were so hypnotic—their brightly colored numbers and animated lines, some of them jagged, some of them rolling in waves, that followed the constant flux of your body, its peaks and dips—and those god-awful warning beeps.

In my dream I'm trying to transcribe the message I've received about the void. Each time I think I'm writing it down I discover that I'm still dreaming, so I write it again only to discover I'm still dreaming—the process goes on and on. I don't know if each transcription is closer to waking or if they're all equally other. I don't know if consciousness operates as a rheostat or a simple on-off switch. When I finally wake up for real, the real feels tentative, a bit transparent. I can only recover fragments, their meaning corroded as Sappho's crumbling swatches of parchment. *Farewell—bride—farewell—much-honored bridegroom.*

Right now I'm eating a walnut half. What do walnut halves look like? My brain on lockdown. Munch munch munch. The more I write to you the less I need anyone else—though for the first time in ages I have friends—real friends. I had to move away from a couple because with my widow vision I could clearly see how fucked up or insincere or unkind the situation was. I won't sully this letter with the details. I give you permission to whoosh into my brain and dig up the dirt. But in general people have been beyond kind, goodness flowing along their skin like opalescent ectoplasm. The last few months of your life, according to my journal, which I wrote in a lot, you didn't exist, not even passing references. After that I write about little else. I've learned to go for days without leaving the house. Because of vaccinations people are gathering more, but I'm even more locked down writing this letter with my scrambled half-a-walnut brain. I only have time for loss and thinking of you. I've becoming a lone nocturnal creature who marvels at this strange phenomenon, sunlight. On the phone I tell Peter Gizzi that the one good thing about lockdown is that I never have to see anybody I hate, which evokes belly laughs from him. During normal times I would have considered this an overreaction, but not now.

I read that matter is perverse, tossing off virtual particles which interact promiscuously with the void. Matter then summons the virtual particles back and touches itself. Emptiness is not empty. It is active, energetic, churning with potential. Wherever you are, I am already touching it. Your fluid relationship to truth— it's like you could see all the possible plots in any situation, and you were loyal to whichever was the most entertaining. As I sit here weak and sleepy, my body gives off sparks that shuttle between being and nonbeing, and I imagine you in the void, your virtual bits caressing my virtual bits, which I fold back into myself as I spit out more virtual bits, seeking out the endless potentials of you. Monogamy was a concept alien to you. You appreciated it as a propellant of narrative through the ages, an ideal to be broken, lied about, killed over. But personally you were indifferent.

When I come into possession of good gossip that only you could appreciate, this is when I get all sloppy with grief. The urge to share is as strong as sex. Recently Hedi was telling me about this person I don't know, who is all about the grand gestures, whose conversation is only about themselves, who seem close for a while then dismiss you. Exactly the type of person you would love— the outrageous stunts, the mistreatment of others, the lying, overstepping, climbing, each new exploit so over the top you can only respond with a laugh. I said to Hedi, "You seem to get involved with an awful lot of narcissists." And he replied, matter of factly, "They're the people who create things." He asked me what I did about all the fans that want attention from me, who want to move into my life. I said that it wasn't an issue. I either ignore them or they like my writing but they don't like me. And then I held the phone in silence, feeling like a dysfunctional dweeb.

According to my social media algorithms, your death was bigger than David Bowie's. Some poets tweeted about your death on and on—how great you were, etc.—and never mentioned me. As if my being your widow meant nothing, as if I had no more right to your loss than any random internet troll. I felt like posting a notice on Facebook—if you want to honor Kevin, be nice to me, that's what he would want. Your status was huge in our poetry/art fishpond. Power suited you, and your charisma soared—but I never stopped loving your earlier iterations. The mess of a popcorn-eating chainsmoking Stephen King fan I fell in love with—he's been dead for years. During a visit to Los Angeles I asked Matias—after thirty-three years of marriage, which Kevin am I mourning? One of us brought up Maggie Nelson's *The Argonauts*, her relationship equals boat metaphor. The boat the Argonauts sailed on was constantly being fixed and rebuilt, until eventually none of its original parts remained, yet it was the same boat. Since people too are constantly changing, eventually the people in a relationship aren't the same people who launched the relationship, yet it too continues to exist. Or something like that. So Matias and I started riffing—the BOAT you and I started out on wasn't the same BOAT as the BOAT later in our marriage—and then you became super gregarious and suddenly the BOAT was full of all these other people—and then after you died some poets wanted to deny I ever was on the BOAT at all. Matias and I grew giddy, giggling like naughty siblings. I asked him—since he knew Kathy Acker for a shorter period of time, if he still experienced multiple versions of her. He said there was the Kathy he knew for nine years, and then there was the Kathy he knew intimately for the last year and a half or two years of her life—the Kathy who desperately did not want to die, who did not accept her death until a week before she died. He said he rarely thinks about that Kathy now—but right after she died, he did all the time.

The longer you're gone the more unknowable you become. Not that I ever felt like I knew you. I recognized you, your preferences, your habits, your eccentric moral code—you were quite predictable, liking the same food, the same patterns, over and over. I used to joke that your aversion to change made you the perfect husband, that you would never leave me. But how the millions of bits of data fit together, I didn't have a clue. I used to say that being with you I learned that you don't have to understand someone in order to trust them. Understanding is overrated. What happens to all the memories of me that are lost with your death? Your own memories, your rewrites of my memories. The sicker you grew, the more invented your memories became. I told Matias about my obsessive googling of frontal lobe tumors—how yours was responsible for your mobility issues—how the doctors told us the frontal lobe is also the location of personality—how you and I said to one another—glad the tumor didn't affect that. But now I wonder—the memory loss, the insatiable socializing, the cartoony behavior where you created a glittery Kevin Killian—more like a character than a persona—how you made up so much. It's like you'd take the barest outline of a story and the novelist in you would flesh out the details. There were recurring character tropes such as the offended diva to whom some bumbler says the wrong thing—and the diva huffs, which you would act out dramatically with your whole body. Sometimes you were the diva, sometimes you were the recipient of the huff. You'd come home flushed with adrenaline, talking loudly with large stagey mannerisms, a sort of stand-up comedian version of yourself. This is what people loved. Matias agreed that a diminished Kevin was still smarter than most people. Your intelligence was freakish, the way some extraordinarily beautiful people's features are so exaggerated they start to look monstrous. Again the question is, who is it that I am missing?

In Season 7 of *Gray's Anatomy*, Callie gets in an accident and is holding on to life by a thread. To approximate her borderline consciousness, the episode is performed as a musical. Characters sing emotional songs, and other characters' responses to them are stylized, overly dramatic. In one of the cleverest sequences, surgeons are in a row scrubbing in for Callie's operation, and their handwashing is synchronized, like a Busby Berkeley chorus line. Laughter leapt out of my throat. For most of the forty-five minutes I cried. Except when I laughed. I realized that laughter and tears aren't opposed but simply different expressions of the same joy, and that I was watching a musical the way you did, throwing open my heart to romance and tragedy. After your heart attack, you fundamentally changed. Your emotional life rose to the surface like a blush, and you could no longer manage stress. You could no longer take care of my endless emotional spasms, which for me who liked being taken care of, was a big loss. Watching *Grey's Anatomy* The Musical I realized that I too have changed. Your death and this aloneness and writing to you has changed me. Writing to you has opened the floodgates. The other night I was thinking about Michael, the first guy I fell in love with, when I was in college, and this one time when we had sex when he had the flu. He was so sick, but at 20 he could rally himself. For just an instant I recaptured my awe at the sheer existence of the long smooth expanse of him. I've been shut down for so long. It's frightening to have changed but not tried, to not know the parameters of my new whatever. I'm sounding like a superhero coming of age story. If I knew how deeply this letter would change my relationship to you and your death, I don't know if I would have begun it. Will the world regain some of its wonder for me? As I texted Pea Culiar, I could teach workshops.

You still get daily spam and group emails that I slowly unsubscribe you from. It's like you never completely left, like you're a radio at an abandoned space station transmitting messages to the void. Scientists on the internet say we're living in a hologram, and I get it, especially when I'm driving. Through the Yaris' windshield I peer at the action on the street around me, impressed with the 3-D rendering. I feel floaty, like the time I took psilocybin in college and was walking down a hill, unable to feel my feet as I hovered a few inches about the ground—Hollywood FX for a saint or a vampire—or a ghost, I suppose. As far as I can tell you are not a ghost and you do not float. You have no form beyond subtle nudges of intuition, and I am such a dull receiver.

Loungewear is the biggest pandemic fashion trend. In the same lounge bra and lounge gown you can sleep/eat popcorn in front of the TV/work in front of the computer. Stick a jacket over it and you can go out to dinner, if you're the type who would brave a restaurant. Jersey jogger pants are similarly versatile. Eric Bakke told me the backside of the jacket he wears for work meetings is full of holes. Which reminds me of false front buildings on movie sets. Which reminds me of a corpse's clothing, cut in a straight line up the back. Which reminds me of shopping for my mother's coffin outfit, how tenderly I chose clothes she would have liked, and then at the funeral her bitch of a sister said to me in the most patronizing, condemning voice—there's no wedding ring on her finger. Something I hadn't thought about, but which was the most important thing to my aunt, and probably the other midwestern wives in attendance. I wore my wedding band for maybe a year after you died. The internet told me that there is no rule for how long to continue wearing it. You wear it as long as it feels right. I planned to never take mine off. But then on Etsy I bought a silver ring set with a tear-shaped kyanite. It was big and blue and sparkly, not widowlike at all. It didn't fit any of the fingers of my right hand, but on the pointer finger of my left it was perfect. I put the wedding ring in a box, thinking about how unthinking I was in doing so.

On Facebook I post a photo from our wedding reception. We look blessed, the spark between us palpable. I think—this picture says we have good sex. Then I wash the dishes, where I think again—I had the most wonderful life but I didn't enjoy it. You wanted to devour the world, and then there was depressed me doing whatever to avoid whatever. More than once have I thought that in a just world our situations would have been reversed. Towards the end you said you worried about me, that neither of us was capable of surviving without the other. You were the most unlikely of mates, but I chose well. Your love was uncompromising and total—I should have been the happiest girl. According to the article "Was I a Bad Wife to My Terminally Ill Husband," obsessive thoughts can be addictive. Sometimes people soothe themselves with behavior that seems miserable—such as compulsively washing their hands—or thinking about the times they were unkind to their dead husband—or that their husband fell out of love with them. I search my memory for evidence of love, evidence of no love. We fought because you wouldn't stop saying yes to people who wanted to come over—I said I couldn't handle it and you said you loved your friends and it meant the world to you to see them. And I realized that my need for privacy, for time alone with you didn't hold a candle to your looming mortality. Towards the end, when the doctors were weaning you off the steroids, and despair was setting in—and exhaustion—you ranted that you didn't care for all these people, it was just an act, and I kept waiting for you to say the unbearable—that you never loved me, that your devotion was an act. But you never went there. I was a pain in the ass, but you never betrayed me.

I have a dream in which the word cathected is central. In the dream I'm connecting with some intimate clothing I haven't taken seriously before—socks or underwear. I remember the word cathected from when I used to read feminist Jungians. It means what I thought it meant: a person, object, or idea is charged with mental and emotional energy. A group of cathected ideas is a complex. Cathexis is not etymologically linked to catheter. According to Freud, cathexis is allocated by the libido. "If mourning is a withdrawal from cathexis, it is inherently a betrayal." Let's pause for moment to take that in. Okay, Freud was a sexist fuckwad, and my gut response is to not give him credence—but this takes the hundreds of pages of grieving I've sprawled across six journals and extracts the essence of my widow's dilemma. Anything I do to survive you is a betrayal. How could anybody possibly reconcile that? Freud is savvy as a cult leader who effortlessly pokes the tenderest part of your psyche and thus you vow to follow them forever. I GO ON. I BETRAY YOU. You could put it on a bumper sticker. Freud used "Besetzung"—an everyday German word meaning occupation. He didn't approve of the hoity-toity "cathexis" as an English translation. "Investment" would have been more in keeping with his tone. Cathexis is now used by New Age types to mean selfish attachment rather than selfless spiritual love. Groan. You said there's no such thing as a good relationship or a bad relationship. You said if you give someone a long enough leash they'll always come back, and I always did. Come back. You convinced me that amorality is the true path to love. I doubt if dead Kevin gives a shit if I move forward or backward. Or sideways. I GO. I BETRAY. I'll always come back.

On *Grey's Anatomy*, Season 3, Episode 12. They intubate George's father, but the tube gets a kink and they have to put in a new one. When they peer down his throat, it's so swollen they don't know if the tube will fit. At a certain point the doctors can tell he's never going to wake up, and his organs are shutting down. Like you, his kidneys are the first to go. George's mother has to decide whether or not to take him off of life support. George says, "He's not Dad like this." When they remove the breathing tube, they don't herd the family out of the room like they did with your sisters and me. They let them stay. The tube glides out and George's father dies in like a minute, no gasping. I'm shaking my head and saying to Netflix—no, it doesn't happen that way.

I dream that each mood I've felt since you died—the painful as well as the pleasurable—has been captured like a genie in its own spice jar, and the jars are arranged in reverse chronological order. This is very important and I have to remember it—but even in the dream I know this won't translate well in the waking world. The dream sums up everything I've been writing to you these past four months. I'm awakened by the doorbell and I run downstairs to get a package. When I return I find my journal, and of course all but the barest outlines are lost. I think: bottled up. I love how obvious and clunky the metaphor is. The dream was about compartmentalizing, about states too dangerous to allow to run free, so they were packed in tiny bottles you reach into with a metal spoon and scoop out a precisely measured bit. The sides of the jars were rounded, like barrels or the giant urns that populate the sets of *The Thief of Bagdad*. The jars weren't standing in an even row. Some of them were lying crosswise. They were arranged both chronologically and in a grid that the more I studied it morphed into a constellation like Capricornus or Aquarius, an ordering that someone more schooled than I could read. I fall back asleep trying to remember more about the jars. I am given a pill. It glows bright yellow and is shaped like a crown. A simple, stylized crown, no elaborate spikes or curlicues. It's similar to the kinetic yellow tooth shape in the painting by Bruno Fazzolari that's on our kitchen wall. The pill is an initiation, that's obvious even in the dream, but to what?

Spice jars = Jack Spicer. Duh. How could I have not thought of that before now? Are you with him? Did he guide you to the gates of poetry heaven? How does he feel about your ashes neighboring his? The spice jars look like urns. How blatant does something have to be to make it through my thick-headed schematics? Jack Spicer: *Mirror makers know the secret—one does not make a mirror to resemble a person, one brings a person to the mirror.* Luke 24:1–4: Very early on Sunday morning the women went to the tomb, carrying the spices they had prepared. When they found the stone rolled away from the entrance, they went in. But they did not find Jesus' body, and they did not know what to think. High above the Thief of Bagdad and his beloved princess sailed away on a flying carpet. Jesus lifted up His hands and blessed them. Then He ascended to heaven, and the disciples lost sight of Him in a cloud.

I looked it up, and yes, the Stations of the Cross is an Easter thing, though not in the fundamentalist Easter that I was raised with. I always felt that not being Catholic I was missing out—on grandeur, on mystery, on a fluffy white first communion dress. Even though my friends who went to Catholic school told me about mean policing nuns who forbid grooming in the washroom because it was vain, so the girls smuggled in combs, tucked in their bobby socks—which sounds more like preparation for a life of prison than holiness. But then there was Audrey Hepburn in *The Nun's Story*, with her huge pure eyes. I first became aware of the Stations of the Cross as something to consider when I saw Russell Fitzgerald's series of fourteen paintings of the stations, with Bob Kaufman as Jesus. They were at the art show that accompanied the Spicer conference at New College, and I remember walking from station to station, enjoying the rituality. Station 1: Condemned. Station 2: Received a Cross. I just found the poster online. The exhibit opened a few days before the conference, on June 15, 1986. Thirty-three years later, on that same day, you died.

There's a Kevin writing folder on the iMac and my laptop, which is backed up both locally and online. I imagine I'll transfer it to any future computers I might own. The hard drive is a crypt, and there is no moving on. I will tend to your needs as long as there is an I to do the tending. Your organizational principles were more spiral than linear, and it's difficult to find any specific piece, so I end up strolling through your files, reading things at random, always surprised. I copied the Kevin folder to a portable hard drive for Andrew Durbin, who's reading it with an editor's eye, searching for uncollected gems. I'm sure Andrew, like me, is also searching for you. He loves you. In your poems, time is both relentless and plastic. From "Cat's Meow":

> I would pull time down
> off the highest shelf
> I couldn't catch it in my fingers
> but on the carpet
> like a spill of salt or sand,
> it would twinkle. Bye.

In my dream I'm walking around our apartment, which looks nothing like this one. It's much larger. Everything is out of place. I go to turn on a lamp and it's on top of a shelf, out of reach. There are tables in the middle of the room, overflowing with tacky stuff. Nothing works. While I was gone you rearranged the room. You messed up my living space, made it all wrong.

In my memory FitzGerald's paintings are vertical; I vividly recollect a thin strip of a painting tightly framing Jesus' lanky crucified body. I thought the paintings had been subsequently destroyed, something about a dumpster and a flood or a fire. I was wrong on all accounts. The Belkin Art Gallery at UBC owns them, and the images I find online are horizontal and stylized, with a limited palette of washed browns and beiges with dabs of blue or salmon pink. Not the gruesome blacks and reds of my memory. I wanted to put *Station 9: Third Fall* on the cover of this book, but I was vetoed. The image doesn't pop enough. It isn't sexy. It looks dated. I suppose all those are true. I make it the desktop picture on my iMac. A featureless woman is in the foreground, exiting the frame. Bee Reaved. Her head is bent slightly forward. If she had eyes, they would be looking downward. She radiates sadness so intense it's blocked out all awareness of the action behind her—you lying on your back on the ground, a dark circle behind your head like an inverted halo. A man wearing a white lab coat is crouched over, attending to you. The intense stripes of white on the righthand side of the painting are reflected in your jacket, making it glow in the muddy room.

Fourteen Stations of a Cross takes place in the North Beach artist bar The Place. In several paintings a poster on the wall announces: BOB KOFFMAN [*sic*] AT THE PLACE IN FOURTEEN STATIONS OF A CROSS. There are tables, people drinking, a bartender, bottles. The series chronicles a figure's collapse through time, falling over a table, being held up by other patrons. Eventually the bar closes and chairs are stacked upside-down on tables. Shapes morph as we move from daily time to mythic time. The poster announcing the series disappears, and the bar becomes darker and more cryptlike. Upside-down chair legs elongate into abstract columns and arcs. FitzGerald's Christ is a drunk who keeps falling down and won't or can't leave after the bar is closed. I've been fascinated with Russell FitzGerald ever since you gave me the tarot deck he illustrated in collaboration with Jack Spicer. I keep it in my top dresser drawer. And his relationship with Dora—her leaving her husband and running off with Russell, a gay man—has felt like a precursor to you and me. I feel very close to you right now. It's fucking unbearable. Suddenly, two angels in dazzling white clothes appear before me. The angels say, "Why do you look for the living among the dead? He is not here."

As I sit on the couch writing this on my laptop, across the room is the suitcase in which Frank O'Hara's manuscripts were stored after he was killed. Donald Allen gave it to you, filled with signed broadsides from the '60s, and I wonder, what the hell am I going to do with all those broadsides. Being your sidekick gave me access to literary legends—from James Purdy to Samuel Delany to John Ashbery and scores more. I got to eat and drink with them, to watch them dance the mambo. I didn't court any of it. You made me lazy. From now on, if anything is going to happen in my life, I have to generate it myself. I don't know if I'm up for it. Frank O'Hara's suitcase is another alien object that I happen to be in possession of but to which I had no right. That's when the panic sets in. All your things are laughing at me, multiplying.

Before you were moved from Redwood City to San Francisco, the nurse supervisor told me that everyone in Neurosurgery thought

Kevin was special. From an email I sent to Michele Carlson, April 19, 2019:

He's much stronger, with the help of a walker, and two physical therapists flanking him, he walked the length of the hallway today, which he couldn't do on Wednesday.

He was starting to irritate me today, which made me think things were getting back to normal. His whole goal, besides being able to work again, is seducing all the nurses. He's the most loved patient on the floor, and he really works to make that happen. He knows everybody's name and gets all these details about their lives out of them. The guy who gave him a sponge bath is named Neil. He's from the Philippines, and he was born in 1970-something and named after Neil Armstrong. And on and on.

You took the virtue of charity to heart, constantly donating to fundraisers. Anybody who said they were in need and asked for money, you sent it. The homeless guy who slept down the street, with white hair and beard, whenever you saw him, you gave him $5. He recognized our car and would stand beside the road, eager, so even when I was alone he got his $5.

I keep thinking of our first visit to Vancouver; I don't know if we were even married yet. It's afternoon when we arrive at Stan Persky's house in Kitsilano. There must have been some greeting and chitchat. Then you and I are in the guest room having sex. It's still afternoon. I don't know how or why we got there. The two of us are frantic on a mattress—maybe it was on the floor—maybe it was a makeshift thing in the living room—I'm pretty sure we didn't plan it—and that I started it. We thought we were being super quiet, but when we got up, Stan was beaming this pervy smile, like we had just given him the best present. The love never left, but that *I have to fuck you right now or I'm going to faint* mode—it's like I'm recalling a 1980s movie—puffy-headed brat rapture in *St. Elmo's Fire*—rather than my own life. Our life. I can almost feel the warmth of your aroused body, a thick radiance I pass through in order to touch you. Though you hadn't begun working on Jack Spicer's biography, he was everywhere—Stan—Robin Blaser—Ellen Tallman—George Stanley—his complicated intimates, his survivors. I'd always thought of history as something you read about in books or went to conferences and heard papers about, but that first visit to Vancouver it felt like I was walking through history, like I could reach out and give it a hug.

The fact that I can gather these memories means you're living again in me. No longer are you a blank absence who withdrew its love.

Years later—August, 2008—we spent an afternoon in the special collections at Simon Fraser University Library. You were examining the Jack Spicer papers that Robin Blaser had recently donated. I was going through boxes of books that were found at Spicer's bedside when he died. They were still uncatalogued, so I typed up a list on my laptop. They were mostly mysteries and sci fi—like you, Spicer's aesthetic was a seamless blend of high and low—and I thank both of you for giving me permission to fuck pretention. Among the cheap paperbacks was *Pass the Gravy* by AA Fair (Erle Stanley Gardner), one of 28 books in his Cool and Lam series. Few of them were in print, but since millions of each had sold, they could be found online for a song. When we returned home, I ordered *Pass the Gravy*, and went on to read the entire series—many of the books gifted by you—at bedtime. It took me a couple of years to get through them all. Night after night as I passed out while holding the battered yellowed paperbacks with their pulpy covers, I imagined the pulse of their previous owners throbbing in my palms. A few of Spicer's bedside books had been published after 1965, the year of Spicer's death, so the sampling was not pure. From you I learned that history is not pure. It's recollections and gossip and preconceptions backed up by sketchy documentation. Your novelistic mindset was perfect for history. When I read *Poet Be Like God* I laugh out loud at your sly wit. Chapter 5, the tragic love triangle between Russell FitzGerald, Spicer, and Bob Kaufman—after you've made it clear that Kaufman wasn't all that into FitzGerald, you use a close third person to move into Russell's head: "He'd hooked Spicer, and felt a very strong affection for him. But the sex they had wasn't as good as the sex he wanted to have with Bob Kaufman." Delightful confounding of lived experience with fantasy. I'm pulled right into FitzGerald's youthful instability, then my gaze turns to Spicer and the futility he must have felt competing against a phantom. I feel your affection for both of them, and I wonder what happens to affection after it's given, does it forever cling to its object or does it shrivel like everything else and die.

The chase buckles us in. We watch who's coming for us through a bullet hole in the broken, spider-webbed rear window. We show real desperation. We cross a line. The chase is about surviving against all odds. "We lucked out, we lucked out!" The chase is wide-eyed in-the-moment immersion. It's heart-throbbing full aliveness, amplified breathing whimpering cursing. The chase choreographs us into the DO NOT ENTER. From our windshield POV, we feverishly dodge cars and semi-automatic fire. The more desperate we are, the more reckless. "Like clockwork, Baby, like fucking clockwork." The chase often begins with a heist. Its beauty is in the editing, not in the stunts.

On *Grey's Anatomy*, Mark Sloan dies. He was never a favorite of mine—attractive in a way I don't find interesting and kind of creepy, a sex addict who falls in love with a girl half his age and somehow turns wholesome. At first it seems like Mark Sloan is going to survive the plane crash. He sits up in his hospital bed, bright and engaged. But all the old-timers—including Sloan himself—suspect he's going through "the surge"—a rush of energy that the terminally ill sometimes get near the end. The former (due to a bout of falling off the wagon) Chief of Surgery helps him fill out an end-of-life directive, like a bureaucratic shaman, and Sloan says if he's unresponsive for thirty days, to pull the plug. Then he collapses. The present of the show is the thirtieth day. When I look up the surge, I find that it's mostly anecdotal, something hospice workers rather than doctors would talk about. One theory is that during the dying process the body releases steroids that stimulate the infirmed. On steroids your favorite word was "beautiful." You'd point to something—often me—and say "so beautiful" with a look of wonder.

Mark Sloan's colleagues/friends/lovers remove his breathing tube and sit with him until it's over. That night in my dream I'm trying to masturbate with a haptic sex toy, but it's not working. Then I turn it upside-down, and the toy melds to my genitals—boom—I am insanely aroused. There's no build up, I'm just there in that moment right before orgasm when you give up effort and relax into it and wait—then the explosion—not the tightly focused clenching of a typical dream orgasm—this orgasm is huge, my multi-pronged clitoris thrashing and convulsing in my pelvis. I am no longer a thing but an essence, sliding back and forth between being and nonbeing. The toy, like my clitoris, looks like a flesh flower, like a deep sea shapeshifter malleable to every oceanic ripple. Mark Sloan is beside me, saying, "That's amazing." It's not my orgasm, but the toy that excites him. The world's best cosmetic surgeon, he's very much into instruments and techniques. My dreams are a repository for the dead. Now that Mark Sloan is dead he can enter them.

For our final wedding anniversary—July 3, 2018—the trendy Italian bistro we were planning to go to was closed, so we crossed Valencia Street and found a French restaurant that seemed perfect—a little fancy but laid back—and only after we were seated did we recognize it. A couple of remodels/iterations ago, this was where we dined when we went on our first "date." It was my thirty-fourth birthday and I wore a lavender jersey dress. It wasn't meant to be a date. My husband was working, so you picked up the slack. We both lived in the neighborhood and had been hanging out—and I'm sure it was fueled by the birthday/Valentine's Day vibe—but this was the first time we couldn't deny that something was happening between us. Returning there by accident decades later felt fated, as if our life together had been encapsulated in a single evening. It was lovely, but it frightened me—as if a too perfect bow was being tied around something that was now completed. I can't remember what we ordered. Or what I was wearing.

And then there were all those commissions we kept being offered those last couple of years that required we collaborate—something we'd long before given up attempting. Your mind was so quick I had to race after it—you'd have a whole paragraph typed before I could even decide what I might want to say. Invariably, we'd struggle for control and end up fighting. It wasn't worth it. But now the ancient Muse Calliope was pointing her finger down from the heavens, booming *this is your final task, to learn to work together.* We still fought—I remember you storming around saying you would never collaborate with me again—but we continued and eventually pleasure outweighed the dramatics, and we took the writing and the exhibition we curated to places that neither of us could have reached alone.

I've been reading Kit Schluter's new poetry collection, *Pierrot's Fingernails*. From "Inclusivity Blueprint": *Now alone, I've lost access to that "redemptive" escape,/ the open and the concealed have swapped spirits,/ and by law you are on a high shelf of transition.* Even though I couldn't suss out a plot or in some passages even a literal meaning, as I read his poems an emotional atmosphere, an intimacy passed through me. It wasn't abstract at all, it was physical with a beat of scary, like an encounter with a ghost. Memory: They didn't take you down the stairs on a stretcher. They took you down on this thing that was shaped like a chair. Memory: In the ER you couldn't recall what month it was but you remembered the doctor's name. I scan my leaky brain for specifics, anything I can use to tart up this letter like the parlor of a nineteenth century century Parisian bordello (see TV series *Maison Close*). All these micro-narratives—all this gaga about this happened then this happened—there's nothing special in—just illness and death via the medical machine in a society that has no mercy for the weak. When you asked the hospital priest to pray for you, Bradford and Peter went teary-eyed. You were here. Now you are not here. I'm here but I don't know what here means without you. That's it. Everything else is fluff and flourish. I wish I could take all the tears I've felt but haven't shed—until recently I've cried very little—and distill them into a perfume. No need to bother with this book. Just one sniff, from nose to brain, POW.

John Ashbery: *I'm sort of notorious for my use of the pronoun "it" without explaining what it means, which somehow never seemed a problem to me. We all sort of feel the presence of "it" without necessarily knowing what we're thinking about.*

When I see you it's rarely the whole picture. Usually you're still, occasionally a burst of gesture. I remember things you said but I can't visualize you saying them. It's like the lens of my memory is stuck on close up. Your swollen shoeless foot. Haze of frustration. Fear. Me trying to reach into that, to help. When I told the ICU nurse about your sleep apnea diagnosis, she burst out laughing. I feel you on one shoulder and Spicer on the other—two perverse angels. The longer you're dead the more I miss you. The early days were filled with anger and confusion. How dare you leave without having resolved every narrative thread of our relationship. I'd weigh instances where you seemed to demonstrate love against that one time in the movie theater when you didn't hold my hand. I've never been able to see love as an ongoing state. Like a child playing peekaboo, when my eyes are covered there is nothing but loss and terror that the love will never return. No lover could have been more consistent and loyal than you. I was the flighty one. Things happen. People do things. I dream that you come back, and we're both excited. You are lying down, kind of groggy, but happy to be with me. I say to you—I've got so much I want to talk about, so many questions. Did you really love me? Did you grow tired of me? Why did you touch me so little at the end? You look at me like the effort to be back is so intense my insecurities don't make sense to you. The first year after you died, your absence was inconceivable, so I tried not to think about you. Now I miss you so much I sometimes feel dizzy. Everything I've loved is being decimated. Zap. Gone. But my love is still here, directionless as a migratory bird that has lost its instincts. If someone's going to die they should take the love with them, not leave it behind, confused. They've even discontinued the Yaris. Toyota killed our car.

Deep Nostalgia refers to AI-generated moving portraits made from photos of the dead. Which image would you choose for your post-mortem animation? There must be thousands. When social media went into its frenzy of mourning, person after person after person posted a photo of themselves with you. You'd be smiling broadly, usually with your arm around their shoulders. It's like you took a photo with everybody you ever met. In Deep Nostalgia the dead roll their heads around, blink ceaselessly. There's something spineless or double-jointed about their movements that has reminded some viewers of the moving portraits in *Harry Potter*. It's like they're floating in a formaldehyde-scented jar of half-life, forever here and not here. All the heads move in similar patterns, and they move too much, like the dead are tweaking or doing some creepy dance to music from Beyond. They look confused, strained, like they're trying to peer out through death jelly. Many of them are a touch cross-eyed. Their movement cycle ends with not exactly a smile. A stiff smirk.

I dream I'm sitting at a sidewalk table at a cafe, on a residential street lined with large trees whose leaves flicker in the sunlight. You pull up in the boxy 1987 Dodge Aries wagon that was part of your signature look, like your pointy turquoise Paul Smith shoes. In 1999 I bought it from Liz Willis for $1,000, sight unseen. It was her parents' vacation car. You spent thousands more on repairs—new engine, new battery, new transmission—and when it could no longer handle the highways you kept driving it around the city, until it finally collapsed from exhaustion. The video you posted on Facebook of it being towed away received hundreds of condolences. The putt putt putter of the engine now sounds more like a purr than a roar. Its pale blue body shines. No more rust, mildew, or broken side vent window. The tattered ceiling fabric which you "fixed" with a staple gun is firm and clean. I'm remembering the homeless woman who moved into the car, threading plastic flowers through the shreds in the ceiling. She said someone sold her the car, and to prove it she showed you one of those pink message slips used in offices. The radio blasts "Where the Wild Roses Grow" by Kylie Minogue and Nick Cave. "And I kissed her goodbye, said 'All beauty must die.'" I wanted to play it at your memorial service, but Bradford said the song was too depressing. The windows are so shiny they're impenetrable, a frenzy of reflected leaves. I can't see inside the car, but I can feel you there, eager to take me for a spin.

The last thing I said to you was, "I love you." You died, and I said it again. *Angels appear in dazzling white robes.* The last word you wrote was "shit." Your right arm was full of tubes, so you held the erasable marker in your left hand and moved it across one of those boards they have for patients who cannot speak, where they can point to their feelings. There was a line drawing of a human body and a long list of words: tired, hungry, afraid, hurt, etc. None of them suited you, so you wrote, in script, with a big flourish on the S: "shit." The last thing I remember you saying to me before they put in the tube, your eyes smiling: "We had a good long run of it, didn't we?" *One breath chases the other. I cannot stop looking for the living among the dead.* The last thing you ate was chocolate ice cream, when we got home from your chemo treatment, when it seemed like you were handling it okay. Then we laid together and I held you, and we both fell asleep. *Angels say, "He is not here."* When we were still newlyweds you crouched over me in this same bed on all fours and said, "I'm your house." Your chest was my ceiling, your cock and balls dangled above my belly. You nibbled my ear, whispered, "This is what you always wanted, isn't it, a house that talks." You acted like sex was a miracle, like I was a miracle that happened to you. But it is you who were the miracle. Bye.

Love,
Bee

Acknowledgments

"Hoarding as *Écriture*" was commissioned for *Ways of Re-Thinking Literature*, eds. Tom Bishop and Donatien Grau, (Routledge, 2018). "Leaky Boundaries" was previously published on the *Artforum* blog, December 2, 2018. Thank you Lauren O'Neill-Butler for being such a dream of an editor and a pleasure to work with. "The Violence of the Image" was written to accompany the photocollage *Stuff My Stalker Has Ordered for Me Online*, both of which were produced for the group show *Trout Fishing in America*, curated by Micah Wood, City Limits Gallery, Oakland, July 15–August 27, 2017. Thank you to Micah for inviting me to take part in the exhibit, and to Casey O'Neal and John Sakkis for inviting me to read my essay while standing next to the collage, an experience I found thrilling. Also, my deepest gratitude to Matt Gordon, who had the technical prowess to actually photoshop and print the collage—and for being such a wonderful friend. "The Pink Place" was written for *Dirty Looks*, ed. Bradford Nordeen, Volume 4, 2019. Bradford—I love writing for you and knowing you in all ways. "The Endangered Unruly" was published in the print issue of *Artforum*, May, 2019. Another shout out to Lauren O'Neill-Butler—there could be more here, but I'll stop at this one. "Laugh and Cry: On Ugo Rondinone's Clowns" was a catalogue essay for *The World Just Makes Me Laugh*, an exhibit of work by Ugo Rondinone, Berkeley Art Museum, June 29–August 26, 2017. Ugo, thank you so much for your generosity and kindness. "Cinderella Syndrome" was written as a catalogue essay for *Ellen Cantor: Cinderella Syndrome*, curated by Jamie Stevens and Fatima Hellberg for the Wattis Institute, December 8, 2015–February 10, 2016; and Künstlerhaus Stuttgart, April 2–July 31, 2016. Jamie, life was so much better in San Francisco the short time you and Patricia lived here. "Pushing and Pulling, Pulling and Pushing" was written as a catalogue essay for *Mike Kelley: Pushing and Pulling, Pulling and Pushing*, 500 Capp Street, San Francisco, November 3, 2018–February 16, 2019. Thank you Bob Linder and Diego Villalobos for providing this fangirl with a venue to write about Mike Kelley. "The Kingdom of Isolation" was written as a catalogue essay for *They*, a solo exhibit by Anne Walsh at the Luggage Store, San Francisco, winter 2018. It was printed in *Hello Leonora, Soy Anne Walsh*, ed. Rachel Churner, no place press, 2019. It was a pleasure and an honor to work with Anne, and to be published in anything by the amazing no place press. "The Ghosts We Live With" was previously published in *Los Angeles Review of Books*, No. 22: Occult, 2019. Thank you Medaya Ocher for inviting me to take part in such a fun project.

"On Becoming Undone" was previously published on the *Artforum* blog, January 4, 2019. "Photo Op" was previously published on the *Artforum* blog, May 14, 2019. "Anniversary" was previously published on the *Artforum* blog, June 15, 2020. Much thanks to Jennifer Krasinski for your kindness and deft editing, and for allowing me a space to publish such personal material. "Jeffree" was previously published in *Frieze*, April, 2020. Thank you Andrew Durbin for "getting" me and for your ongoing friendship and support. "Kevin and Dodie" was first published by Semiotext(e) as a not-for-sale chapbook that was handed out at Kevin's memorial service at SFMOMA, August 25, 2019, which is so above and beyond, I don't know where to begin. It also was included in *Dodie Bellamy Is on Our Mind*, ed. Jeanne Gerrity and Anthony Huberman, Semiotext(e), 2020. Anthony and Jeanne—you changed my world. "Bee Reaved" was a commissioned work of "experimental fiction" for the catalogue accompanying *The Making of Husbands*, the Christina Ramberg exhibition curated by Anna Gritz, KW Institute for Contemporary Art, Berlin, September 14, 2019–January 5, 2020. Much thanks to Anna and to Krist Gruijthuijsen for providing me with the space to begin to work with my grief. "Plague Widow" was written for *diaphanes*, Issue 10—Punk Philology, edited by Donatien Grau, October 2021. Donatien, thank you for inviting me to take part in such great projects.

Special thanks to Donna de la Perriere's close critiques of the Bee Reaved pieces. And for the glory of her and Joseph Lease's friendship.

And then of course there's Semiotext(e), the best publisher imaginable. Thanks to Chris Kraus for continuing to believe in me. And to Hedi El Kholti—without you I would not have been able to survive this book or the past two years of my life. Much love to you.

ABOUT THE AUTHOR

Dodie Bellamy's writing focuses on sexuality, politics and narrative experimentation, challenging the distinctions between fiction, the essay and poetry. In 2018–2019 she was the subject of *On Our Mind*, a yearlong series of public events, commissioned essays and reading group meetings organized by CCA Wattis ICA. With Kevin Killian, she coedited *Writers Who Love Too Much: New Narrative 1977–1997*. A compendium of essays on Bellamy's work, *Dodie Bellamy Is on Our Mind*, was published in 2020 by Wattis ICA/Semiotext(e).